SPIRITUAL
LEADERSHIP

BILL McRAY

SPIRITUAL
LEADERSHIP

Leading God's Way

BILL McRAY

spiritual leadership
LEADING GOD'S WAY

First Printing 1996

Second Printing 2007

Revised 2010

Copyright © 2009 by Victory Fellowship Publishing

A Victory Fellowship Church Publication

ISBN: 9780982682203

Victory Fellowship Church

P.O. Box 100885

Nashville, TN 37224

615-254-3322

Table of Contents

Introduction

In the church world, leadership principles have been neglected for a very long time. In these last days, the Lord is speaking to our neglect. Pastors and other church leaders are showing a great interest in the subject of leadership, and well we should, for according to Ephesians 4:11-12, training up leaders is a primary function of the five-fold ministry. Without trained leaders in the Body of Christ, it becomes impossible to perfect the saints for the work of the ministry. Whether you are a member of the five-fold ministry, or are in some other area of church leadership, or not even in leadershp at all, I believe the leadership principles shared in this book will help to better equip you for wherever you serve in the Body of Christ.

Leadership, particularly in the secular world, has many images. Some see leadership as a place of exalted position. Some see it as a means to control and manipulate other people. Some even see leadership as a vehicle to establish their worth as a person. Leadership opportunities have been desired for all these reasons and more. In the following pages, I want to share with you how I have come to see leadership after thirty years of pastoring a local church. I have found that the Word of God has a great deal to say about leadership in the local church. If we study closely the life of Jesus, we discover that He spent much of his time and energy in the training and development of His disciples. After all, it was into these men's hands that He knew He would place the responsibility of the building of His Church.

In Mathew Chapter 16, Jesus proclaimed that He would build His Church and the gates of hell would not prevail against it. He said that He did not intend to stick around and build it with His own two hands and His own leadership skills. Instead, He chose to build His Church through the power of the Holy Spirit working through otherwise ordinary men and women. Therefore, His public ministry to the needs of the people was only a part of His earthly mission. That is the part that we have majored on through the Church, as we should. However, Jesus was not only the greatest minister of all time, but He was also the greatest developer of all time. He took twelve common, unlearned men and developed them into the great Apostles of the Lamb.

The incidences of training and development in godly leadership principles abound throughout the four Gospels. Many readers have missed them either because they had no interest in the subject or they did not know what to look for. Most people never thought of Jesus' ministry in this way. But just as leadership training was a major part of Jesus' ministry, it must also be a part of ours. The LAST DAYS REVIVAL is upon us, and it is going to take a host of leaders to oversee the greatest of all harvests.

There are two kinds of people in the world: followers and leaders. Both are of equal importance. Without followers, leaders have no reason for existence. Without leaders, followers accomplish nothing. Where two or three are gathered together, you must have leadership. The purpose of leadership is to bring order and to give direction. Leadership's purpose defines its responsibility. To fulfill its responsibilities to bring order and give direction, those responsiblities must be accompanied by the authority to fulfill them. The purpose of authority is to fulfill responsibility. Authority is never given to leaders to lord it over God's heritage. It is given only to equip them for bringing order and giving direction.

With these simple truths as a foundation, I invite you to examine the following material with a heart to serve as a godly leader in the Body of Christ. Revival has come to our land, and with revival will come the harvest. We must equip the saints for the work of the ministry. We must have wise and godly leaders. We must not lose the harvest.

CHAPTER ONE

Servanthood: The Heart of Leadership

The night before His death on the cross, Jesus and his disciples were in Jerusalem celebrating the Passover feast in a setting that is now referred to as "The Last Supper." It was a very intimate time for all of them — one of the most intimate times that we find recorded in the Bible.

Probably the most vivid account of this night is given in the Gospel of John, chapters 13 through 17. In these chapters, Jesus gave His disciples significant instructions that they would need in order to carry out His work on earth.

He shared many things in those few hours, and one of the things He did was to lay down a standard for effective godly leadership. The principles He defined are ageless and apply to leaders today just as they applied to the twelve disciples. If you desire to become an effective spiritual leader, you must hear and understand what Jesus said and did on that night.

John 13:2-17

2 And supper being ended, the devil having now put into the heart of Judas Iscariot, Simon's son, to betray him;

3 Jesus knowing that the Father had given all things into his hands, and that he was come from God, and went to God;

4 He riseth from supper, and laid aside His garments; and took a towel, and girded himself.

5 After that he poured water into a basin, and began to wash the disciples' feet, and to wipe them with the towel wherewith He was girded.

6 Then cometh he to Simon Peter; and Peter saith unto him, Lord, dost thou wash my feet?

7 Jesus answered and said unto him, What I do thou knowest not now; but thou shalt know hereafter.

8 Peter saith unto him, Thou shalt never wash my feet. Jesus answered him, If I wash thee not, thou hast no part with me.

9 Simon Peter saith unto him, Lord, not my feet only, but also my hands and my head.

10 Jesus saith to him, He that is washed needeth not [except] save to wash his feet, but is [entirely clean] clean every whit: and ye are clean, but not all.

11 For he knew who should betray him; therefore said he, Ye are not all clean.

12 So after he had washed their feet, and had taken his garments, and was [seated] again, he said unto them, Know ye what I have done to you?

13 Ye call he Master and Lord: and ye say well; for so I am.

14 If I, then, your Lord and Master, have washed your feet, ye also ought to wash one another's feet.

15 For I have given you an example, that ye should do as I have done to you.

16 Verily, verily, I say unto you, The servant is not greater than his lord; neither he that is sent greater than he that sent him.

17 If ye know these things, happy are ye if ye do them.

This act that Jesus performed upon His disciples has a number of different meanings. For instance, there is a great principle having to do with forgiveness of sin for the believer which restores fellowship with God. There is also a great teaching here about people forgiving each other and walking in forgiveness, love and harmony with one another.

There is another principle also illustrated which is the foundational key to leadership. It is the principle of servanthood, the attitude that must accompany leadership.

There is a passage of Scripture that occurs several times where the disciples are arguing among themselves about who would be the greatest among them, who would have the highest position, who would have the greatest role of leadership, and which of them would be exalted above the others.

When Jesus overheard their argument, He began to chastise them. He called their attitude the attitude of Gentiles. (The word Gentile is generally used to refer to the world's system, or in this case, natural leadership.) Jesus told the disciples that Gentiles desired to rule over one another. In other words, the world's system of leadership exalts the leader above the follower in order for the leader to have control over his followers.

In Mark 10:43-44, Jesus said that they must follow a different rule: *"But so shall it not be among you: but whosoever will be great among you, shall be your minister: And whosoever of you will be the chiefest, shall be servant of all."* So, according to true godly leadership, a leader is to serve. We hear politicians use that terminology all the time about serving the country, serving their constituency, and serving the people. No doubt there are some people who honestly and genuinely run for office in order to serve and to make a contribution. On the other hand, I believe there is a more significant number who run for the fulfillment of their own purposes and ambitions. Jesus clearly stated that the motivation for leadership is servanthood. He said if you want to be the greatest, you *must* be the servant of all.

Let's look at an example which shows that Peter had learned this lesson well. In 2 Peter 1:1, Peter introduced himself to those to whom he was writing. He called himself *"a servant and an apostle of Jesus Christ, to them that have obtained like precious faith with us through the righteousness of God and our Saviour Jesus Christ."*

Peter identified himself first and foremost as a servant, and then he mentioned his spiritual office. Notice that he did not place his office above his servanthood. He served as an apostle, but he did not see his apostolic calling as a place of natural exaltation above other men and other women in the Body of Christ. He saw it as a position of service to the Lord and to the people. This is the way we should all look upon the position of leadership. Its purpose is not to obtain a position of exaltation above others, but rather to serve.

The literal translation of the word *servant* in the Greek is *slave*. Peter literally said, "*Simon Peter, a slave and an apostle of Jesus Christ.*" When he said that, he was saying, in effect, "*I have no life or identity of my own.*" He had laid down his life for the Master. Jesus had taught him well. For Jesus said that if you want to save your life, then give it up. Peter had willingly done that.

Think about the condition of a slave. A slave has no personal rights. He is not allowed personal ambitions or personal fulfillment. He doesn't have significant personal identity. A slave is looked upon as a non-person existing for one purpose and one purpose only, and that is to serve his master. Most of the time people were made slaves by force, but Peter was identifying himself in that role by his own choosing.

Jesus Christ, the Head of the Church, made Peter an apostle, but Peter made himself a slave. This is very important in our understanding of servanthood and leadership. God may choose to make you a leader, but you must make yourself a servant. This principle is borne out in Philippians 2:5-11:

> *5 Let this mind be in you, which was also in Christ Jesus:*

6 Who, being in the form of God, thought it not robbery to be equal with God;

7 But made himself of no reputation, and took upon him the form of a servant, and was made in the likeness of men;

8 And being found in fashion as a man, he humbled himself, and became obedient unto death, even the death of the cross.

9 Wherefore God also hath highly exalted him, and given him a name which is above every name,

10 That at the name of Jesus every knee should bow, of things in heaven, and things in earth, and things under the earth;

11 And that every tongue should confess that Jesus Christ is Lord, to the glory of God the Father.

Verse five says to *"let this mind be in you, which was also in Christ Jesus."* If you study the word *mind* here, you will find that the Greek translates mind as "attitude". It could read, "Let this attitude that Jesus had be in you." Or, have the same attitude that Jesus had.

What was Jesus' attitude? In verse six, Paul writes, *"Who, being in the form of God,"* meaning in the fullness of, or having the essence of deity, fully equal with God in every way, in every attribute. Jesus possessed all the divine qualities and characteristics of the Father. He had the full essence of divine glory, lacking nothing, being fully and completely and altogether equal with God the Father in every way.

Jesus did not consider it overstepping His boundaries to be equal with God, but He did not hold on to that equality. Why? Because of His attitude of servanthood. In His leadership role as the Son of God, He was there to serve those over whom He was Lord. And He was there to serve God.

A leader always has someone above him (unless you are talking about God, Who is the only exception) and the followers below him. The leader is called to be a servant of both—to serve those above him and to serve those who are below him in position.

The Scripture says, "*He (Jesus) made Himself of no reputation.*" Don't you think He had a pretty good reputation to give up? Isn't it interesting that Jesus was not born the son of a king when He was born in the earth. He wasn't born into the most influential and wealthy family of the nation. He wasn't born among the elite. He was born literally a nobody, the son of a family whom we would consider to be common, ordinary people. This was God's choice. He made Himself of no reputation and took the form of a servant. We are talking about the Ultimate Leader of all Leaders! Jesus was and is the greatest of all leaders other than God the Father, Himself, to Whom Jesus is equal. And yet He became a servant and was made in the likeness of men.

Identifying with the Ranks

Jesus took on the form of a servant and became like those He served. No leader is fit to lead anyone unless he is willing to be like them. If you are not willing to get down in the trenches with those who follow you and become like your followers, then you have no valid grounds for leadership. Jesus, the leader of all, was willing to be made in the likeness of men. A leader can not see himself as superior or greater than those who follow him if he wants his leadership to count at all.

Jesus humbled himself and became obedient to the call and the task at hand. He was willing to pay the ultimate price to accomplish what needed to be done, even the death of the Cross.

We are talking about the motivation for leadership. The world doesn't look at leadership the same way Jesus does. Remember the way the disciples were arguing in Mark 9:34: *"For by the way they had disputed among themselves, who should be the greatest."* They were saying, "I'm going to be greater than you. I'm going to have a higher position than you. I'm going to be president of this outfit someday." If we think of leadership in natural terms, we will see it as a place of self-exaltation and a place in which others will serve us. That's also one reason many followers resent leadership and authority. They see authority as oppressive and they see leaders as controlling masters. In these cases the attitudes are wrong, both in the area of leadership and among the followers.

Let God Exalt You

Because Jesus made Himself a servant and became obedient unto death, God exalted Him. In spiritual matters, things pertaining to the Kingdom of God, and even in this natural life, we must submit our destiny into the hands of God. Then when promotion comes, it will be from God, not from man. That's why the Scriptures exhort us to be God-pleasers and not men-pleasers.

Why is it that people seek to please men? The truth is they want to be exalted by man. The Scriptures, however, exhort us to please God. If we refuse to be men-pleasers, that doesn't mean we are to be contentious or unfriendly, but we are to walk in love with all men to the greatest extent possible. It means that we mustn't look to man to put us over, we must look to God.

God exalted Jesus. If we do the same thing that Jesus did, if we have the same mind and the same attitude that He had, and follow the same principle that He did (both spiritually and naturally), then God will exalt us also. We must remember that exaltation (or a more modern word - *promotion*) comes from God, not man. 1 Peter 5:5 very clearly states this:

> *5 Likewise, ye younger, submit yourselves unto the elder. Yea, all of you be subject one to another, and be clothed with humility: for God resisteth the proud, and giveth grace to the humble.*

Pride has been the downfall of many a leader. The prideful person will find himself resisted by God.

Humble Yourself

This Scripture continues in verse 6 with a key that shows how you can expect to receive promotion from God.

> *6 Humble yourselves therefore, under the mighty hand of God, that he may exalt you in due time.*

Humility is up to you. It is a trait that we ourselves must determine to have. You have heard it said that if you don't humble yourself, others will humble you, or God will. That is not true. Other people may *humiliate* you, but only you can *humble* yourself. There's a big difference between humility and being humiliated.

Humbling yourself under the mighty hand of God is like seedtime and harvest — give and you shall receive. The same principle is involved. Humble yourself and God will exalt you. Enter into pride and God will resist you.

King Saul is a prime example of this principle. When God chose Saul to be king, He looked at his heart and found him to have the heart that He desired in a man. Saul was a humble young man with the right spirit and motivation about him.

Remember in 1 Samuel 10:21, we are told that when the time for his coronation came, he hid, and they had to look for him. As you follow Saul's life, however, you see that he did not continue to be humble. It didn't happen suddenly, but very gradually. This is the way life works, and this is the way the curse works. This is also the way people's attitudes change.

The change in Saul's attitude occurred so gradually, there is no doubt he didn't even notice that he was becoming a different man. Very gradually he ended up prideful, arrogant and with an ungodly attitude of self-interest. He became very selfish, jealous and resentful, and because of this, he became very insecure. As a result, he ran headlong into God's resistance. You can read that everywhere Saul turned, God resisted him and his pride.

Under the Mighty Hand of God

When we exalt ourselves, we fall. But when we humble ourselves under the mighty hand of God, we succeed. What does it mean to humble ourselves under the mighty hand of God? What is His mighty hand? It is His leadership and His authority.

Anyone who has authority over you in any area also has responsibility *for* you. Once you understand this, it will set you free in a lot of areas. You see, authority has only one purpose and that is to fulfill responsibility. So in every area in which God has authority over your life, He has responsibility *for* your life. When you humble yourself under His mighty hand, you are yielding to His power and authority to fulfill those responsibilities in your life. That is why Paul says we are to submit to those who are in authority over us because they have the responsibility for us. God has designed the order of authority to be a blessing to us.

Selecting Leaders

Leadership has been established for our good. Our government leaders, for instance, are to be a blessing to us. If we would see them as such and pray for them as we ought in all things and select them as we ought, we would see a lot more blessing than we do.

People often select leaders, whether in government or not, for the wrong reasons, just as people often become leaders for the wrong reasons. In far too many cases, a leader is chosen who will best serve one's personal interest. That's why we often hear of people who vote "according to their pocketbooks". Instead of voting for the most qualified leader, many vote for the person whom they believe will give them the best economic advantage. These people are selecting leaders based on their own perceived self-interest.

We need to select our leaders based on the principles of God's Word and whether or not the candidates measure up to those principles. By doing this our nation would become very different.

We should select leaders according to whether or not their hearts seem to be right toward God and toward the office of leadership they want to fill. The key factor by which we can judge someone who wants a leadership position is by his attitude toward servanthood.

The Depth of Servanthood

Throughout the Gospels you will see that everything Jesus taught, He performed. He taught servanthood, therefore He demonstrated servanthood. As we read in the beginning passage of our study, *"He got up from the table, the Lord of all, removed His outer garment, girded Himself with a towel and began to wash the disciples' feet."*

In light of the culture in which Jesus was a part, this was an act of the lowest ranking servant in the household. Only the lowest servant was given the duty of washing people's feet. That is why Peter protested when Jesus began to wash his feet, saying, *"You are going to wash my feet? Never!"* He did not understand the principle that Jesus was teaching. He just saw it as an act unworthy of the Master. Jesus answered him by saying, *"If I don't wash your feet, you don't have any part with Me."*

Jesus was performing a natural act, but He was explaining a spiritual principle. It applies to us today just as it applied to Peter and the disciples then. Even though we have been made the righteousness of God in Christ, we are still in the flesh. We are not yet perfected. Therefore, when we walk through this world, we often get our feet dirty. Our acts of sin overtake us at times. This dirties our feet. When it happens, we are to follow the instructions of 1 John 1:9 and let Jesus wash us clean. We are told, *"If we confess our sins, he is faithful and just to forgive us our sins, and to cleanse us from all unrighteousness."* He tells Peter while He is washing his feet, *"If I wash you not, you have no part with me."* In other words, unless we allow Jesus to cleanse us from our sin, we can have no fellowship with Him.

When we allow the King of kings to wash our feet, we are truly humbling ourselves under the mighty hand of God. Stop and think about this for a minute. Jesus does this as an act of service. God's forgiveness of sin is an act of service to us on His part. When He forgives us, He is literally serving us. When Jesus went to the cross, it was a service. He shed His blood for all mankind.

Every act of God's grace is an act of service. When He extends His grace, it is not as the exalted Supreme Being extending an act of benevolence. Don't get me wrong. It is definitely a benevolent act that only God can perform. But that's not the attitude with which He does it. His attitude is foremost and always the attitude of serving.

13

Every time you go to God in repentance and say, "Oh, God, I missed it. Forgive me," Jesus girds Himself with a towel and kneels down before you, just as the lowliest servant would, and washes you clean of that sin. Every time you ask for forgiveness, that is what you are asking Jesus to do. You are asking Him to gird Himself with a towel, get down on His knees and wash your feet. And He delightfully does it because He sees His position as the Head of the Church and Lord of all as a place of service. Because of this humility, God has *"highly exalted Him and given Him a name above every name--the name at which every knee shall bow and every tongue confess that He is Lord."*

This is the motivation for leadership. It is not to be exalted above others, for if you exalt yourself, you will fall. If you enter into pride, God will resist you. But if you humble yourself, He will give you grace. If you humble yourself under His mighty hand, He will exalt you in due time, just as He did Jesus. So let this mind be in you (let this *attitude* be in you) that was also in Christ Jesus.

CHAPTER TWO

Natural Leadership

There are two kinds of leadership, natural and spiritual. They are very different and yet both have similar attributes. The difference between the two is how they function. Natural leadership functions, or is exercised, through enforcement. Spiritual leadership is exercised through relationship.

In this world there is no such thing as pure spiritual leadership. It must contain some factors of natural leadership. This is because we are spiritual beings living in natural bodies, and we have to deal with both elements. We cannot say that one form of leadership is right and the other is wrong, but we can say that one is more effective than the other. Spiritual leadership is far superior in effectiveness than natural leadership. Why is this true? And how can the two successfully work together in the Church and in other areas of our lives? One of the secrets is knowing how to employ the principles of spiritual leadership in natural things. When you learn to do this, the results can be very powerful.

Jesus identified the two forms of leadership in Matthew 20:25-28. He focused on the difference between the two and the way they are exercised when His disciples came to Him seeking appointments of leadership.

> *25 But Jesus called them unto him, and said, Ye know that the princes of the Gentiles exercise dominion over them, and they that are great exercise authority upon them.*
>
> *26 But it shall not be so among you: but whosoever will be great among you, let him be your minister;*
>
> *27 And whosoever will be chief among you, let him be your servant:*
>
> *28 Even as the Son of man came not to be ministered unto, but to minister, and to give his life a ransom for many.*

In verse 25, Jesus described the method of exercising *natural* leadership. In verses 26-28, He explained how to operate in *spiritual* leadership. Before we can understand how spiritual leadership can be implemented into our natural lives, we must first know the principles of natural leadership.

Government Leadership

One of the best examples of leadership in the natural realm is government. The purpose of government is to bring order and give direction to society. Notice I did not say its purpose is to control society. Yet the tendency of any form of natural leadership is to assume more and more power over its jurisdiction. This is certainly true of government, isn't it?

In our country the founding fathers formed a government for the people, of the people, and by the people. The Constitution of the United States of America was originally set up with the intention of having as little interference in the lives of the people it governed as possible. Unfortunately, over the 200-year history of our nation, we have seen that drastically change. Not only has our nation and its population grown, but the government has also grown. It is now by far the largest employer in the nation.

As the size of government has increased, the more involved it has become in the lives of the people. Along with increased involvement, the government has assumed more and more control. This is not something that came about as a sinister plot of a group of people set out to control this country. No, it wasn't a conspiracy. Nor was it a particular political party attempting to take over. It was something that occurred very, very gradually. It happened in what I believe was a genuine effort by our government to fulfill its function and meet the needs of the people.

If you think about it, all natural leadership tends to increase its involvement in the lives of the people whom it leads, until it begins to control the direction and order for their lives. Eventually, it becomes a problem, as it has with the United States government. We can readily see that our government has become so involved in the lives of the people, that many legislators are looking for ways to curtail it. This is why we hear all the talk about downsizing government. Even with its problems, though, government is still the best example of natural leadership.

How Government Operates

Government demonstrates the principle of leadership by enforcement. The way government brings order and gives direction is first of all to pass laws. In the United States, the government leaders draw up and put into place what is called a Body of Law. Its purpose is to regulate and order some form of society. Once legislated, it then becomes the responsibility of society to live in obedience to the Body of Law that is laid down for the benefit of the whole.

There may be certain laws that are inconvenient to some individuals, and because of the inconvenience, those individuals may choose to violate the laws. However, doing that is not in the best interest of society as a whole. Therefore, it becomes necessary to enforce the law. In order to do that, the government has set up arms or branches of government for the purpose of law enforcement.

Every city in the United States has its own law enforcement agencies that are established to maintain order. Nashville, for instance, has become quite a metropolitan city, with people from all over the world. With all these different cultures and classes of society, there is tremendous diversity, and because of this, governing Nashville has become increasingly difficult, making the enforcement of many of our laws necessary.

If everyone lived honest, upright, godly lives, there would be no need for law enforcement. Unfortunately, that is not the case. All you have to do is pick up the newspaper or turn on the television news, and you will find that every single day people are violating laws by shooting, killing and robbing. You name it, it is being done.

Since we need a law enforcement agency, our government has set up a police department to enforce the laws. What happens if you violate the law? The police come along to enforce that law and either put you in prison or fine you, whichever is relative to the infringement that has occurred. Because of the consequences of breaking the law, most people choose to obey the law.

If there was no repercussion for robbing banks, we would see it happening a great deal more than it does. For instance, if someone had a need for money and the pressure got bad enough, even though he may not have a criminal mind, that person might go down and rob a bank, law or no law. People would just help themselves to what they needed. So, you can see that leadership by enforcement is necessary. As we can see, natural leadership is necessary in this natural world, but it is limited. Its limitation stems from its ability to enforce.

Limitations of Enforcement

This is how the limitations work. If I am a natural leader, leading by enforcement, as long as I am present or have an agent present to carry out my leadership responsibilities and enforcement, then the desired end result will occur.

For example, if you are driving down the highway and you know that there are going to be three speed traps between you and your destination, but you do not know where these traps will be set up, guess what you are going to do? You are going to drive very close to the speed limit all the way to your destination.

What will happen if you need to get somewhere in a hurry? Let's say you are a little late and you know that there are no speed traps on that stretch of highway and little enforcement. Most likely, you are not going to be as conscientious about observing the speed limit as you would be under the other condition. If the enforcing body is present to enforce the leadership, the result is obtained. But if enforcement is not present, neither is the desired result.

Most people, even church leaders, rely on leadership by enforcement. If you are one of those, then you are always going to be limited in getting people to do what you desire of them, simply because you will always have to be present to cause it to happen. Natural leadership, as necessary as it is in a flawed society and in a flawed world, is extremely restrictive.

Communism

Communism is a perfect example of the limitations of natural leadership. The Czech Republic, for example, was under the rule of communism from the end of World War II until when the Wall came down. Since the Wall, or the Iron Curtain, fell and the Czech Republic became its own nation and free again, there have been tremendous changes. It is now an open society with a totally different structure.

Under communism, all the people lived and carried on separate lifestyles, for the most part, in the confinement of the neighborhoods in which they lived. They did not have supermarkets or department stores, or any of the modern-day conveniences that people in many other parts of the world take for granted.

Here in the United States, you are able to buy all your groceries in one place. Not so under communistic rule. Each neighborhood had its own little individual shops. You had a meat shop, a bread shop, a vegetable shop, and so on. For every need, you had an individual shop, and in each community the same structure was duplicated. Each community was isolated within its own neighborhood society, and its people learned to function in confinement.

In order to leave their community and go to another part of the city, people had to have special permission. Each citizen was also encouraged to inform on his neighbors, so people didn't carry on conversations with one another or socialize with others. They minded their own business because they assumed everyone else was an informant. People could get their neighbors into a great deal of trouble simply by lying. They would literally inform on folks if they saw them drop a piece of paper on the ground, or for any other infraction.

What was this all about? Control — enforcing the control of the leading authorities. God never intended government to be oppressive, but to be a blessing. Government was to benefit, not oppress. The point of my illustration is to show the extreme lengths that some governments have gone to in order to make sure its will is enforced upon the people so they could be controlled.

A communist society was a totally controlled and manipulated society. It was so much so that the older generation in the countries like Czechoslovakia, who grew up and lived under communism, are finding freedom very difficult. Many of them, as unbelievable as it may seem, would like to go back to the old system because under it they did not have to take responsibility for their lives. Under communism the older generation would have gotten a meager pension, but all that is gone. There is no longer provision for them, and they literally do not know how to take care of themselves.

Under communism, the government provided the barest essentials. You were not allowed to own property. The government provided rental housing, and everyone worked. Everyone. You did not have a choice. The government assigned jobs, most of which were "make work, do nothing" jobs. Everyone also had food. As basic as those provisions were and as low a quality of life as they lived, many of the people became accustomed to having everything done for them. They did not have to fend for themselves.

Responsibilities of Freedom

Certainly freedom presents problems, and one of these is that with freedom comes responsibility. The more freedom an individual has, the more individual responsibility he has to take for himself. Under communist rule, the government assumed responsibility for everyone. It owned everything and regulated everything. Sure, you did not have to take responsibility for yourself, but you were allowed no choices and no individual authority.

On the other hand, in a democratically governed society, the only responsibility a government has over its people is that which the people allow. In order to accomplish its goals, the more responsibility a leader is given, the more authority must accompany that responsibility.

Within this system, we, the people, have turned the United States government into what is called "big government" with big government programs. Every one of the programs that has been instituted by the government, good or bad, workable or not, is a responsibility that has been given to the government by society. We have voluntarily turned the responsibility over into the hands of the leaders.

In order to remain a free society, we must understand the consequences of relinquishing responsibilities. The more responsibility a leader is given, the more authority he also has been given. That is why freedom-loving people should never give its leaders any more responsibility than is absolutely necessary to accomplish the things that individuals cannot do for themselves. For instance, individuals cannot enforce the laws. Vigilantism would be the result and we know that individual retribution does not work. We would end up with every man doing what seems right in his own eyes. Instead, if we see someone breaking the law, we do not attempt to arrest that individual, we report him to those to whom we have designated that responsibility.

There are other things that we cannot do. As a nation we cannot defend ourselves individually against foreign governments. Our nation has to be defended, but we, as individuals, are powerless to do it. Yet we need a defense system. Therefore, we have turned over that area of our responsibility to the government. The government in turn has formed a military branch whose primary function is to enforce the sovereignty of this nation by defending it against encroachment by any other nation.

Some nations use military power not just to defend their own nation but to infringe upon the sovereignty of other nations in order to overtake and control them. We, however, as a democratically governed nation and a freedom-loving people, would probably never do that. When we give up any area of responsibility, we are relinquishing a measure of freedom. Also, when we turn over responsiblity plus the authority to enforce it, we obligate ourselves to submit to that particular responsibility and authority.

An example of this would be having to go to war for our protection. Then the government would enact the draft. Let's say a young man receives his notice that he has to join the military. He doesn't have a choice; he has to go. If he does not, the enforcement agency will come and get him, exercising their authority of leadership. If the young man refuses to submit, he will ultimately go to jail. Why? Because this is a necessary responsibility that society has delegated to the government.

A Fragile Nation

There are other areas where governmental authority is absolutely necessary. The infrastructure of the nation, for example, belongs to the government. The roads, streets, sewers and all the utilities--all the things that make our lives so livable in this country--fit into this category. Relinquishing the authority to take care of this network is necessary. These needs make our lives so very, very fragile. All it would take to paralyze a city is to cut off the electricity. If this were to happen, few of us could function without making radical changes.

Weather conditions, such as ice storms or hurricanes have created such situations. We have learned the hardships. We have all these wonderful gadgets such as light switches, heating units, and such. You can just turn a button and heat comes on. That is until your electricity goes off! Then what happens? Do you hang a pot of beans over the fireplace?

Our society could be shut down in a moment by simply turning off the gas, electricity and water. All the responsibility and authority for these things have been placed in the hands of the government, because we have determined that government can supply them much better than the individual. The alternative is to go back to cutting down our own trees for wood and digging our own wells and building our own streets.

Our nation came forth through the hard work of rugged, hardy, individualistic people who were the pioneers of this great country. They cut themselves a piece of life out of the wilderness. Today, we are surrounded by these wonderful conveniences, none of which I want to do without. Nevertheless, we must recognize that with a higher standard of living, we have been made extremely vulnerable. The more comfortable we are and the more livable our society becomes, the more fragile it is, and the less individualistic our people are.

The framework of our country works by enforcement. We have relinquished not only the responsibility for it, but also the authority. When the bill comes, you pay your electric bill or your electricity is cut off. You obey the speed laws on our streets or you will receive a fine or be put in jail.

Property taxes would be another example. You are required to pay taxes on your property or the government will confiscate it. You may have your own property in our nation and you can do anything with that property you want to within certain guidelines. The government has created the guidelines because society has decided that for the good of the community, we must regulate what people do with their property. Yet in making that decision, we gave up a certain amount of individual freedom.

Understanding Both Realms

Do you see how natural leadership works? Interestingly enough, this is also the way spiritual leadership works. The same principle applies to both. In any area in which we relinquish responsibility, we give up authority in that area.

When people understand these things, it's easier for them to submit to the authority of leadership. By the same token, it is just as important for leaders to understand the principles as it is for followers. A leader is not to become a tyrant, demanding submission, but he or she is to be someone whose purpose is to fulfill the function of leadership, by bringing order and giving direction.

CHAPTER THREE

Spiritual Leadership

The goal of a good leader is to get people to do what he wants them to because they want to and not because they have to. Once you are able to do this, you have found the key to the success of spiritual leadership. It is called leadership by relationship. This is not to say that enforcement is never required in spiritual leadership, but you will find that the majority of spiritual leaders will exercise their authority through relationship rather than enforcement.

The Power Base

The first step a spiritual leader must take in fulfilling the responsibilities that he has assumed is to establish a power base. The power base, whether natural or spiritual, is the seat or core of a leader's authority. It is where authority originates. The only power base a spiritual leader has is his relationship with those whom he leads. Therefore, he must establish his power base by establishing a relationship with his followers.

Let's look at how natural leadership establishes a power base. Throughout history, you can see examples in nations that were ruled by kings. When a new king was appointed, he immediately sought to establish and solidify his position so that he could reign securely in his kingdom. The common practice, whether the kingdom was inherited or taken through a political or military overthrow, was to eliminate everyone who had been in power before. They were either banished or killed. This included not only those who had been in power, but anyone who might be perceived as a threat against the new regime in the future. It was not uncommon for a new king to have his brothers and all his family members killed because he saw them as possible threats to his kingdom.

In most civilized countries today, this does not occur in the sense that enemies are exterminated. Politically, however, they are eliminated just the same. In our country, when a new president is elected, the first thing he does is clean house. He brings in a whole new cabinet and a new administration. He is still doing the same thing kings did, just using more civilized methods. He is establishing his power base. In order to be a successful leader, this is necessary.

You cannot rule in the presence of opposition. That is, you cannot rule your own kingdom with people around you who are opposed to you. A leader is completely dependent upon his followers if he is to fulfill his duties, so he must have their full cooperation and support.

You may be surprised to know that presidents, governors, mayors, or leaders in general, do very little themselves. They are usually the visionaries or planners. Others take hold of their leader's ideas and directions and they are the ones who carry them out. Because of this, it is necessary for the leader to be surrounded by people who will hook up with him. If they will not do that they must be replaced. Where a natural leader enforces his plans by eliminating opposition, a spiritual leader will rely on another method. He will establish relationships.

The Pastor Illustration

The role of a pastor is one of the best examples of how the principles of spiritual leadership should be implemented. However, the principles apply to anyone who has responsibility for any group of people whether it is a large group or a small one. He may be a head usher in a church, the leader of a prayer group, or a business executive. It is easiest to follow the role of a pastor, however, because he is the most obvious spiritual leader.

Let's say a new pastor takes over a church. As pastor, his leadership role is two-fold: he must operate as a natural leader, but he is primarily involved in spiritual leadership. His *authority* however, is mostly spiritual with only a very limited degree of natural *authority*. For example, a pastor has little power of enforcement, but he does have the *responsibility* to bring vision and direction and he must keep order. He also has the responsibility to feed, train and develop the sheep spiritually and to minister to their needs.

How does he do all this without the authority or power of enforcement? He accomplishes it in several ways: through the ministry of the Word, through prayer and by his own example. The people follow him because of their relationship with him. This requires a faithful congregation. In order for any church to be effective, or even exist in the first place, it must have a faithful congregation. No pastor can be successful without that essential component.

Faithful in what way? For one thing, the congregation must be faithful in finances. The church cannot exist without money. If you have buildings, you must maintain buildings. If you have staff, you must pay salaries and benefits. You must also pay utility bills, not to speak of the money required to provide the ministries necessary to meet the needs of the members and their families.

How do people become faithful givers? They must be taught to tithe and give offerings. This is an area of the pastor's responsibility. Still, he has no authority whatsoever to enforce tithing and giving offerings any more than he has authority to require people to come to church on Sunday mornings. His responsibility is solely to teach his people the importance of faithful attendance and service to God. If they come, it is because they decide to come. Faithfulness in tithing and giving offerings is brought about the same way--by a decision, and that decision is the member's, not the pastor's or any other leader's. The only *authority* the pastor has been given is to teach the truth of what God has said. That is why Paul declared in Acts 20:17-27 that he was free from the blood of all men. He was telling the church of Ephesus after his last visit that his responsibility for them was completed:

> *17 And from Miletus he sent to Ephesus, and called the elders of the church.*
>
> *18 And when they were come to him, he said unto them, Ye know, from the first day that I came into*

Asia, after what manner I have been with you at all seasons,

19 Serving the Lord with all humility of mind, and with many tears, and temptations, which befell me by the lying in wait of the Jews:

20 And how I kept back nothing that was profitable unto you, but have shewed you, and have taught you publickly, and from house to house,

21 Testifying both to the Jews, and also to the Greeks, repentance toward God, and faith toward our Lord Jesus Christ.

22 And now, behold, I go bound in the spirit unto Jerusalem, not knowing the things that shall befall me there:

23 Save that the Holy Ghost witnesseth in every city, saying that bonds and afflictions abide me.

24 But none of these things move me, neither count I my life dear unto myself, so that I might finish my course with joy, and the ministry, which I have received of the Lord Jesus, to testify the gospel of the grace of God.

25 And now, behold, I know that ye all, among whom I have gone preaching the kingdom of God, shall see my face no more.

26 Wherefore I take you to record this day, that I am pure from the blood of all men.

27 For I have not shunned to declare unto you all the counsel of God.

Paul said that he was not responsible if they failed or succeeded, because he had declared the full counsel of God to them. He knew it was his responsibility to teach them, but he also understood it was not his responsibility to live their lives for them. He was not responsible for their faithfulness to put the things he taught into practice.

Free Choice

Each individual is responsible for himself and his own life. A pastor has the spiritual responsibility and oversight for his congregation as a whole, but not over the individual lives of the members of that congregation. No pastor, for instance, can have a relationship with God for a member. Whether a member is faithful, obedient, or applies the Word in his own individual life is that member's responsibility.

If the pastor of a church was to be responsible for the Christian lifestyle of his church members, then God would have given him authority to require them to live according to the Word. He would be able to enforce attendance, tithing and service in the manner of the Communist government. But a spiritual leader does not have the authority to do that. Again, his responsibility is to declare the whole counsel of God and to spiritually minister to the people and their needs. He accomplishes it through his relationship with the people, as Jesus Himself, clearly demonstrates.

Jesus is the Supreme and Sovereign Head of the Church. Yet, He exercises virtually no natural enforcement upon the church. People must follow His leadership voluntarily. He spilled His blood and paid a dear, dear price so that we could be saved, but He does not force salvation upon any one of us. People die and go to Hell every day and Jesus allows them to do so—not because He doesn't love them, or because He has not provided salvation for them, but because He values their freedom to choose. None of the things of God is forced upon us. We serve Him out of a desire to do so.

Establishing Relationships

So, the spiritual leader, having little natural ability to enforce anything, must set up his own power base by establishing relationships. The most important trait a spiritual leader should have is the ability to establish relationships. The quality of the relationships that the pastor has with his sheep (or the leader has with his followers), determines the quality and effectiveness of his entire ministry. His power and ability to accomplish and fulfill his responsibilities are all dependent upon that relationship.

How do you develop a leader/follower relationship? First of all, you must understand the difference between relationship and fellowship. Relationship implies a connection, or linking together, where fellowship implies familiarity, companionship and intimacy.

As a pastor, if you start out with just a few people, you can, and probably will have, fellowship with every member. You will know them and all the members of their families. You will know their situations and circumstances very well. This is true in a business as well as it is in the church. You can only do that when your numbers are small, but having a strong pastor/ sheep relationship does not necessarily require having close fellowship with each individual. Once your group has reached any size at all, you lose the ability to maintain intimacy. It is still possible, however, to maintain close *relationships.*

God is capable of establishing a supernatural bond between the pastor and his sheep whether he even knows their names or not. Size of the congregation does not matter. It can occur with the pastor of a church with thousands, or hundreds, or dozens of people.

There are different levels of intimacy in relationships, but not different levels of spiritual bonding. If every church will believe God for that and submit itself to that spiritual bonding, it will take place. Unfortunately, some congregations do not understand the principle and want to keep their numbers small in order to maintain their close fellowship.

Levels of Authority

Here again, Jesus gives us an example to follow. The Scriptures tell us that He is no respecter of persons, yet we learn that He had different levels of followers. Out of the multitudes that followed Him, He chose, under the inspiration of the Holy Ghost, twelve men to become intimate disciples. As we learned earlier, the purpose for choosing those twelve men was not for companionship, but to train and develop them so they might go forth and build the church after His death, burial and resurrection.

Many people have gotten the impression that Jesus spent His three years of ministry on earth going about with twelve men. If you study the New Testament closely, you will discover there were more likely 70 or 80 people with Him most of the time. As a matter of fact, most scholars believe this larger group traveled with Him everywhere He went. Many of them, we are told, were women from Galilee who ministered to His needs and to the needs of the rest of the company. Jesus had many disciples, but the twelve were the ones with whom He developed the most intimate relationships. These men were able to experience a very close and personal relationship with the Messiah - the world's Spiritual Leader. Even so, Jesus did not love a single one of them more than He did those others whose names we do not know.

Out of the twelve, Jesus chose three - Peter, James and John, whom He drew into an even closer intimacy. It was these three that He took with Him on special occasions such as the Transfiguration in Matthew 17:1, and when He raised Jairus's daughter from the dead in Mark 5:37. Why did He choose them and not the others? Because, at the same time He was developing the twelve to become leaders of all the followers, He began developing these three to become the leaders of the twelve.

In training and ministering to large groups of people here on earth, you have to break things down into more workable components in order to accomplish anything. It is not so in the spiritual realm. There, every believer has equal access to the throne of God. However, when Jesus walked the earth, He walked as a natural man, and every person could not have equal access to Him.

By the same token, every member of a congregation does not have equal access to the pastor. It is not because of favoritism or anything like that. It is simply that the people who have the greatest access are those who work the closest to him in the ministry of the church. The intimacy of relationship is determined by the position people hold in leadership. The church staff, such as the Sunday School Director, Helps Minister, or Music Minister will have closer access than the member who attends church on Sunday morning. At the same time, the pastoral staff, such as the Associate Pastor, Youth Minister, and Children's Minister, will have a closer relationship with him than the rest of the church staff.

It stands to reason that you are going to know your pastoral staff members better than you know the rank and file members in the church because you spend more time with them. For the most part, church members must make appointments to see their pastor--not because he is so important, but because of his natural limitations. Again, this is not true in the spiritual. God is not limited by any kind of restrictions. You do not have to make an appointment with Jesus. He is always available, and no one has any more influence or favor with God than you do. But as long as you are operating in the natural restraints of the earth, you will be required to lead through varying levels of intimacy.

Spiritual Bonds

You begin to establish your power base the same way Jesus did. You surround yourself with a select, dedicated group of people who support you. Their level of intimacy with you will be determined by their role in your ministry, but your relationship with them does not have to be personal in order for it to be strong and effective.

When I went to Rhema Bible Training Center, I did not know Kenneth E. Hagin, the founder and president of the school. God supernaturally told me to pack up my family in Tennessee and move to Oklahoma to attend Rhema. I knew who Brother Hagin was, but I had never heard him preach, or even read any of his books. I was strictly following the leading of God to go.

The first time I ever laid eyes on Brother Hagin was the day he walked into the first class. Even then, someone had to tell me who he was. For many years after I graduated and returned to Tennessee, I still did not know him. The whole time I was in school, I never met him personally, and never spoke to him other than to say "hello" in passing. He didn't know me from Adam. But during all those years when we had no personal relationship, we still had a relationship. It was a close bond formed by the Holy Ghost.

Brother Hagin didn't know me at all, but I knew him. The bond between us was so close that he became my mentor. He was my spiritual father long before he ever knew my name, or before there was any kind of personal relationship between us. It was something that happened supernaturally as I sat under his ministry.

This is the same thing that happens between a pastor and his congregation, or between any leader and his followers. When the pastor stands before his congregation to minister to the people, he doesn't have to take everybody out to dinner to have a relationship with them.

Far too many pastors have burned themselves out trying to have intimate fellowship with every one of his members. It used to be that you could do this because life was much simpler. The congregations were generally small and the members lived in close proximity to the church. The people were also at home a lot more than we are today. It was a different era then.

Even if we were able to spend that kind of time together today, it is not necessary. The natural contact is not what establishes the relationship. Natural contact produces natural relationships. Thank God for the intimacy of personal fellowship. But the people that you are closest to have no stronger spiritual bondage with you than those that are not. Whether you have a congregation of twelve or of thousands, you can still minister to them through that same bond, and they will follow you because of the spiritual relationship.

We have also known pastors who have tried to lead their people by enforcement. The element they always use, without exception, is fear. This kind of pastor tells his congregation that if they don't tithe, they will perish, or if they don't come to his particular church, they will go to hell. These are extremes, but they occur. Many leaders are more subtle than that. Since they have no natural authority to enforce their will, or what they perceive to be God's will, they resort to manipulation and control. This is nothing more than spiritual witchcraft-- controlling other people through fear.

But the pastor who understands leadership by relationship will count his congregation as his sheep. As their shepherd, he will lead them, not drive them, and through the supernatural bonding from the Holy Spirit, they will follow.

CHAPTER FOUR

Giving Direction

You may have heard the statement, "He is a born leader!" It is true that there are people born with certain giftings (or talents) and abilities. Those people may be born with great potential to lead, but they are not born leaders. There is no such thing as a born leader. Good leadership skills are acquired through a great deal of training and experience just as other skills in life are.

No one is born a great physician, or a great attorney, or preacher. A person may be gifted in one of these professions or callings, but in order to be successful he must receive training and experience. At the same time, there are many extremely qualified physicians, attorneys, or preachers who are not successful in their professions. The same is true with leadership. There are other things in addition to giftings and training that determine a successful leader. One important factor is the ability to give direction.

Leadership versus Management

A successful leader must understand the difference between being a leader and being a manager. A leader is the one who gives direction. Giving direction and giving *directions* are not the same. Giving direction is setting a course, which is done by a visionary. Giving *directions* is implementing and managing steps by which the course is followed. Management is an important part of leadership, but a manager is not necessarily a leader. He may not be a visionary who gives *direction,* but he can be the one who brings order to the plan. At the same time, the leader may not be a good manager, but he must *have* a good manager in order to achieve his desired results. The ideal situation is to have someone at the top who can do both, but sometimes it takes a combination of gifts to fulfill what is needed.

If I owned a business and did not plan to run it myself, I would find a good manager who could take my vision and implement it. I would not look for an entrepreneur. If I brought in a visionary to manage my business, it would not be long before it would become his business. What I would need is someone to keep order and follow the structure and direction that I would give. In this case, you have one individual who is a visionary giving direction and another who takes the direction and fulfills the vision.

Very simply stated, the visionary (or leader) is a direction-giver. The ability to give direction or impart a vision is absolutely essential to good leadership. Without it, the leader can go nowhere. He may have a plan, but if he is not able to give direction for fulfilling it, his plan will stall. He may be able to maintain his status for a while, but there is a principal in life that says if you do not make consistent, steady progress you will begin to decline.

Another principal to keep in mind is that it is a lot easier to *obtain* than it is to *maintain*, and since it is not easy to maintain, then it is even more difficult to make continual progress. Once a leader has obtained a position, he must maintain it by continuing to move toward the fulfillment of his ultimate vision.

The Vision

Just what constitutes a vision? The Bible tells us in Proverbs 29:18, *"Where there is no vision, the people perish."* So obviously a vision is of extreme importance. The word *vision* is used a number of different ways, especially in the Bible. Sometimes when the Bible speaks of a vision it is talking about an experience such as Peter had in Acts 9:43. We are told that while Peter was praying on the housetop, he had a vision. He saw into the spirit realm. But that is not the kind of vision that is referred to in Proverbs. It is not saying that unless everyone has a divine vision and sees into the spiritual realm they are going to perish.

The vision that this scripture refers to is purpose, direction, goals, and meaning. In other words, it declares a reason for being. A nation must have a vision, or it will not survive. A local church must have vision, or it will falter. Vision is what Jesus gave to the Church. He brought this great vision and imparted it to His followers.

A leader must start with vision. One of his major responsibilities is to obtain vision, purpose, direction, and goals. He must first grasp the reason for being and then impart it to the followers who in turn fulfill the vision.

In the same scripture passage in Proverbs, we also have the word *perish*, which is an interesting word. We should not just accept our preconceived understanding of the English language when it comes to the Bible. We need to study and search out meanings. "Perish" is one of the words that can be greatly misunderstood.

Normally when we use the word *perish*, we mean to destroy or obliterate. Perish in this particular scripture, however, does not mean that. Here, it means "to become unbridled." What it is referring to is a lack of control, or lack of discipline. The scripture is saying that without a vision the people will become undisciplined and run wild.

What happens when a horse is unbridled? It runs wild. Whatever he wants to do, he just does it. But when a horse is bridled he can be given direction to go wherever the owner wants him to. I have ridden horses for years, but I am not going to put a saddle on a horse, climb on his back, and just let him take off without a bridle. I would not advise anyone else to do this either. I intend to keep control over the direction in which we go.

The same holds true with people. If a leader does not have a vision, the people will not be able to accomplish the things he wants them to because they will be out of control. It is the responsibility of leadership to keep order, but without a vision it is very difficult. It can be done, but it will not be successful. There are certain methods that can be used to control people and maintain a certain level of order for a limited time. But, if the people do not have a purpose or reason for remaining as a group, or have a common bond to keep them together, they will start drifting away to do their own thing. They will become unbridled.

Vision keeps us focused. It gives us direction and purpose and lets us know where we are headed. It also helps us understand our goals and what we are out to achieve. Vision is necessary regardless of the type of leadership involved.

If a doctor has a medical practice, he must give vision to it. He cannot just drift along. He must know where he is headed and what his goals are. He needs to identify the purpose of his goals and what they are going to accomplish. Without this vision, his practice would just drift along, and as it drifted, it would steadily decline.

The same is true with a local church. Lack of vision is one of the reasons that the vast majority of local Christian churches in America never get beyond a hundred members. The average membership in the thousands of churches in America is one hundred people. Most local churches never break a hundred and only a small percentage goes beyond two hundred. Those that have five hundred or more members make up less than one percent.

Hireling Pastors

The more a church grows, the better able it is to fulfill its greatest potential in the community. Most churches that do not grow lack leadership because they are pastored by hirelings. The word *hireling* means a person who follows orders for pay — a hired hand. (Now don't jump to conclusions until I have presented the whole picture.) In most cases, it is the church, and not the pastor, who makes him a hireling.

What do I mean by that? In many churches in America, the pastor stays only a few years. Therefore, the church never has adequate leadership because it is constantly changing pastors. The pastor barely has time to get to know the people, much less get a vision for the church. And if he does get a vision, he may be hindered from carrying it out by a committee, a board, or the congregation.

The Word of God does not give us specific direction for a godly step-by-step form of church government, only guidelines and principles. Therefore, we have several different forms of church government. The most common example is the congregational governed churches, such as you find in the Baptist churches, Church of Christ, and Assembly of God. Whoever is the governing body is the head or supreme authority over that church, whether it be the congregation, the pastor, or a board.

In a congregational form of church government, the congregation is the leader, not the pastor or even the board. In actual practice, it is usually the board of deacons, or more likely, the chairman of the board of deacons, who runs the church. There is no such thing as a group of people leading anything. It always comes down to one man or one woman who exercises the ultimate influence. That is just the way leadership works. Different forms of church government just provide different methods to obtain a single leader.

If you study the Bible you will find that this is the way God always worked. Any time He wanted to do something, He never looked for a committee to do it. He always found a man or a woman to accomplish what He wanted. When He wanted to make a covenant and draw out a people unto Himself, He found a man, Abraham. When He wanted to judge the world, but save a remnant, He found a man, Noah. When He wanted to liberate Israel, He did not go to the elders. He found Moses. You can follow this pattern right down the line. When He brought the nation of Israel into the promised land, He appointed judges, both men and women. When He wanted to speak to the people, He anointed prophets.

When Jesus established the church, He did not change the pattern. He did not say *we* will build *our* church. No, He said *I* will build *My* church. In any endeavor there must be one head, someone with ultimate responsibility. Therefore, someone must have the highest authority, not for the purpose of dictation and overrule of everything, but to accomplish a goal.

Another form of church government is authoritarian leadership of which the Catholic Church is an example. The ruling force in the Catholic Church begins with the Pope and continues down through the Bishops, Cardinals and Priests. In this particular government, the congregation has virtually no say whatsoever in what takes place in the local church. It has no voice in selecting its Priest, or the direction of the church. This is a hierarchy type of church government - a bishopric form of government run by the chief bishop, who is the Pope.

Then there is the pastoral form of church government, which simply means that the local church is headed up by the pastor. There are exceptions to everything. For the most part, the churches that have the greatest vision, accomplish the most, and impact their communities, are the ones who keep a pastor for an extended period of time.

A church can accomplish its purpose with any form of church government. Most do not do that however, because the pastor is unable to get his vision accomplished under congregational, board or committee rule. He must contend with too many variables. Either someone in the congregation is upset with him, or someone of the board disagrees with him. Sometimes he becomes frustrated and leaves. Whatever the reasons are, the pastor is made a hireling, and usually nothing is accomplished.

There are wonderful exceptions. All forms of church government can work, which is why God has not given us a specific one. There are different needs for different communities. What is required is for people to operate according to the Word of God, walk in love, and follow the Holy Spirit.

A Matter Of Trust

One of the greatest men of God in this country or in the world pastored a large denominational church in one of our large cities for over 40 years before retiring. His church made a great impact on their city. The pastor was a man of vision and purpose who was able to fulfill his leadership role through the confidence that his people placed in him. Throughout his years of ministry, the members learned his character, his integrity, and his trustworthiness. They committed and submitted themselves to him as their pastor. It did not happen overnight. It usually takes a leader at least five years to truly become the pastor of his church because it takes time to establish the relationship from which to lead.

In this church, the pastor operated under the umbrella of a denominational leadership. Through its form of government, a pastor was allowed to use very little of his natural authority. For instance, he did not have the authority to approve a budget or to purchase land. The congregation was the ultimate authority, voting on everything. But the person who actually ran that Dallas church was this particular pastor. Whatever he approved, the congregation approved. Why? Because they trusted him. That does not happen unless a pastor has been with the church long enough to gain the people's confidence and respect.

There have been other cases in which the leader has taken the people's confidence and abused it. A leader has no right to expect anyone to follow him blindly, or just accept his leadership at face value. No pastor ever gets to the point where his leadership performance is not measured by the Word of God. In 1 Corinthians 11:1, Paul said, *"Be ye followers of me, even as I also [am] of Christ."* He didn't say, "You follow me because I am the great apostle with all the revelations. I know what is right and you must follow me." Instead, he persuaded them with the truth and exhorted them to follow him as he followed Christ. Paul established his leadership through months and years of proven performance.

God never intended for pastors to move from church to church, leaving churches with constant turnovers that hinder progress. Roaming pastors break every leadership principal in the book including the first, which is to bring vision. The vision, whether in business or in the church, can only come from the head. It never comes from below and filters up; it always comes from the top down. The vision is not given to the church body, or to a board or committee. You will not find an example of that anywhere in the Bible.

God did not give the vision for deliverance to the people of Israel. In fact, they did not even want to follow the vision He gave Moses. They were a rebellious, cantankerous bunch, who eventually came together as a mighty nation through a leader with vision. Still, it took Moses forty years to get them across a river that they should have crossed within a few weeks.

God has given us apostles, prophets, evangelists, pastors, and teachers. It is the pastor that He has called to head up the local church, and it is to that man that He gives direction and vision. It is the responsibility of the leader or pastor to get with God in prayer so that he can get the vision and direction for his ministry. It is then his responsibility to impart the vision to his congregation of followers, in order that together they can fulfill their part in building the Kingdom of God.

CHAPTER FIVE

Shared Responsibility & Delegated Authority

To be an effective leader of a large organization, you must rely on two key factors: shared responsibility and delegated authority. The leader who tries to do everything himself will never be the leader of anything very large. That is not to say that an organization must be large to be effective or meaningful. Often smaller organizations are more effective and of higher quality than some larger ones. This is especially true of churches.

Success is not measured in size, but in effectiveness and in impact. Unfortunately, too often we have measured the success of a church by how many people it ministers to for two hours on Sunday morning. This is hardly relevant to true success and effective leadership. Nevertheless, many of us today believe we are on the threshold of the greatest revival that has ever been which will result in the greatest harvest of all time. If this is true, we must learn to lead masses of people. This can only be done through shared responsibility and delegated authority.

Too Big For One

The purpose of leadership is to bring order and to give direction. Order comes through organization and direction comes from vision. In the church, vision comes from God to the senior pastor. The pastor is charged by God to lead the church into the fulfillment of the vision He has given. He cannot do it alone. A true vision from God is always bigger than the man or woman He gives it to. It is greater than what a person can accomplish alone or without God's help. Therefore, he must be able to share the responsibility and delegate authority. A leader who is too insecure to share and delegate will never fulfill his vision unless it is a very small one. If the leader's vision is small, it did not come from God, especially in the end-time harvest.

Imparting the Vision

The first responsibility of leadership, to bring order, has been fairly well fulfilled in the church. Organization has not been the problem in most cases. Imparting vision, however, has been a challenge. That is where most leaders falter for several reasons, most of which center around a failure to share and to delegate.

Moses is one of our greatest examples of this failure. In Exodus 18:13, when his father-in-law, Jethro, came for a visit, he found Moses judging the people from sun-up to sun-down. His work was a noble and necessary work. There was nothing wrong with what Moses was doing. His failure was in trying to do it all himself. Jethro watched him for a very long time and then basically said, "What you are doing is not good. You are wearing yourself and the people out." He then advised Moses to appoint responsible and qualified leaders to help him with his task. Moses heeded Jethro's advice and appointed leaders of tens, leaders of hundreds, and leaders of thousands. Thus he multiplied himself many times through shared responsibility and delegated authority.

I am convinced that one of the reasons most churches in America number under one hundred members is because their leaders make the same mistake Moses was making. The work these pastors are doing is a noble and necessary work. They are just trying to do too much of it by themselves. Some may not know how to share and delegate well. Some may be too insecure to do it well, and some may be such perfectionists that no one can do the work to suit them. The latter's motto is "If you want it done right, do it yourself." Whatever the reason, the result is the same. In these cases the only part of the vision that gets done is what the leader can do himself. If Moses could not do it, why should we think we can?

Methods of Impartation

In the local church, the primary way the pastor gives direction is through the impartation of the vision God has given him. God has a specific vision for every local church. Many aspects of a vision will be the same for every church, but some aspects will differ. There are basically two ways a vision is imparted. The overall vision must be imparted to the congregation by the pastor from the pulpit. This will, of necessity, be very general in nature. The specifics of a vision must be imparted by the pastor to specific people. This latter group will be his leaders. One leader or group of leaders will receive one part of the vision and another leader or group of leaders will receive another part. These leaders will in turn hand down even smaller parts to those under them.

You cannot force-feed a whole cow to a person at one time. One would never invite guests to his home and serve up a whole cow on the table. He may tell his guests, "We are having beef for dinner," but his guests are not thinking cow. Instead, they are thinking steak or prime rib. Even then, when a fine steak or cut of prime rib is set before them, they are given a knife and fork to cut it into bite size portions. You can take a whole cow and feed a large group of people, but even then it must be rightly proportioned, giving the appropriate parts to the appropriate people. Some like steak, some like roast, some like hamburger. So it is with a vision. We cannot serve up the whole thing at once and expect it to be imparted. It won't be. Some people are equipped for one part and some for another. Shared responsibility is serving up various parts of the cow to the appropriate people for fulfillment.

A vision should begin with the pastor and through shared responsibility and delegated authority spread down through the various layers of leadership until it feeds the whole congregation with purpose. The person who retains everything to himself and tries to do all the work is the same person who is trying to feed the whole cow from the pulpit and wondering why he can't motivate his people with his vision. This does not mean that he cannot be a good leader, but his leadership will encompass only the space that he is able to fill himself. In order to fulfill our vision, we must rely on other people. No one person can do it all.

Unique Skills Required

Not only is one person unable to do it all from the standpoint of time or location, there is no person, regardless of how talented or good his leadership skills, who knows how to do everything that needs to be done. There are all kinds of things that must be accomplished that the pastor personally will not have the skill or knowledge to do. A good leader will not even try to know everything. The leader should be as knowledgeable as he can be, for sure, but he, himself, is not required to accomplish his goals. All he needs to do is find people who do know how, share that portion of his responsibility, and delegate the authority necessary to fulfill it. He should also have the good sense not to meddle with his people while they do their part.

When a leader shares responsibility and delegates authority, he is not abdicating either. Delegating means to share the responsibility with others. Abdicating is divesting oneself of that for which he is responsible. When the leader shares responsibility and delegates authority, he simply multiples himself so that much more can be accomplished.

CHAPTER SIX

Leadership by Multiplication

How does a leader multiply himself? First of all, there is a difference between multiplying oneself and duplicating oneself. Multiplying yourself is not a matter of function and personality so much as it is a matter of ability to perform. In order for a person to work well under another person, the two do not have to have the same personality. They don't have to have the same ways of doing things. They simply have to be able to grasp the leader's vision, hook up with it, and carry it out according to their own personality and way of doing things. That's the difference between multiplication and duplication.

Of all the people who serve in the ministry of Victory Fellowship Church, there is not one who is anything close to a duplication of me as the pastor or leader. They are all, however, multiplication of my leadership.

Some leaders want everything done their way. They not only want to supply the vision, but they want to supply the detailed plan of operation as well. What you end up with is a "cookie cutter operation." Everyone is forced to do everything the leader's way under a specific, detailed, operational plan. This just puts people in straight-jackets.

There was an individual who once worked for a well-known pastor. Someone asked if it was difficult to work for that particular pastor. He answered, "No. It's not difficult at all. It's real easy to work for him. You just do everything his way."

Actually, it is much more difficult for a person to do things the way another person does. Each person is unique, and when a person is forced into another's pattern, he is not able to reach his highest potential of ability. He simply becomes a mimic of someone else's methods. Success comes from learning how to impart vision to people and then allowing them to share responsibility for the portion that has been delegated to them.

This is the most effective way to get things done. In order to successfully do this, a leader must understand human nature. He must start by selecting good quality people or he will end up with a mess. Either nothing gets accomplished or things get accomplished that you do not want.

There is a balance. You must be able to give people the freedom to do things their own way, using their own methods and personalities without ending up with separate little kingdoms within the ministry. Otherwise, you do not have a team, you have a bunch of individualists doing their own thing.

An organization must be a team, working and flowing together. All the pieces must fit together like a good puzzle without being forced and without bad joints. If you have a situation where you have certain people who are building their own kingdoms rather than fulfilling your vision, then you run into problems.

The major factor in developing people and getting things done in a manner of excellence is through your relationship with them. If you depend upon your relationships then people will do what you want them to because they want to do it, not because they are required to do it. As we have shared before, leadership by enforcement is a very valid form of leadership in the natural, but spiritual leadership must rely on relationship.

Taking Charge Without Taking Over

In order to get people to do what you want them to do because they want to do it, a leader must learn how to take charge without taking over. A take-over kind of leader is a micro-manager, or a person who wants to have all the input. He not only supplies his vision, but he lays out the plan of operation to implement the vision. He is always looking over shoulders, making sure everyone is doing things according to his own methods. This is a person who has not learned how to take charge without taking over, and it causes a lot of tension and resentment. When you take over, your people will feel forced. But by taking charge, you don't force people. You inspire them.

It is difficult for a micro-manager to keep good people who have many gifts and abilities, because they are stifled. It is one thing to become subordinate or submissive to a leader, and this is good and necessary. It is another thing altogether to be required to relinquish one's gifts and abilities. A good, quality, gifted person will eventually break out in order to express his own gifts and abilities.

There is a way to take charge without taking over, allowing people to grow and even helping them to develop their abilities. Our personalities are interwoven with our giftings and abilities, and when you learn to allow people the freedom to creatively express themselves, you can keep them for as long as they are supposed to be with you. Usually, when a person leaves under these circumstances, it is not a result of their frustration from being stymied or boxed in, but because God is moving them.

When you observe a constant turnover of people, you can many times trace it to a micro-manager. This kind of leader is not able to keep long-term people, not only because he is difficult to work for, but because people are not allowed to grow and develop into what God has created them to become. Instead, their leader is trying to recreate them into the image of himself. Those who do stay under those circumstances usually lack ambition and motivation. They stay because they feel safe in this type of environment. Nothing is required of them and they have few responsibilities.

Effective people must be allowed to develop. Development can occur without compromising your own goals and purposes. It is more important for a job to be accomplished well than for a job to be accomplished the way you would do it.

Efficient Or Effective?

In the ministry of the local church, effectiveness and efficiency do not always go together. As a pastor, I am not so much concerned with efficiency as I am with effectiveness. I want people to be effective, and they can't always be effective and efficient at the same time. An efficiency freak has a very difficult time pastoring and operating in spiritual things, because spiritual things are not driven by the natural, and efficiency is part of this natural world.

God is very efficient, but He is efficient in the overall spectrum, not necessarily in specifics. For example, God gave Adam a wife and set him in the Garden of Eden which was full of all manner of fruit trees, loaded with fruit. Let me ask you a question. How much fruit can two people eat? If God was efficient, He would only have put two or three trees with just a little fruit on each one, enough for two people. But that is not what God did. He was more interested in effectiveness. His plan was to create a garden of abundance.

In leadership, effectiveness is far more important than efficiency. That's why I am not a real strict, hard-nosed individual when it comes to the exercise of people's time. It doesn't bother me to walk into staff members offices and see them sitting there reading the Bible or a magazine or something else. I consider that a part of their becoming effective. Natural efficiency, however, would demand that they demonstrate productivity--pounding on computers, running to and fro, doing something every minute of the day. Some pastors I know expect that kind of atmosphere. What they end up with is a lot of efficiency, but little effectiveness. Of course you cannot allow lack of efficiency to become slothfulness. There is a balance between effectiveness and slothfulness. You can get in the ditch any way you go. Some people tend to become slothful when they are not rigidly regimented.

I am not a regimented person, and I don't require it of my staff. However, I am somewhat habitual. For example, when I get ready in the mornings, I go through the same process every single morning, exactly the same way unless there is an interruption. I follow a pattern. There's a reason for that. The reason is that there is great liberty and freedom in a pattern. When you follow a pattern, you don't have to think through each step and your mind is free to meditate on other things. In the mornings, I am free to meditate on the Scriptures, or my day, or to pray. In the hour or so that I spend getting ready, my mind is completely free.

If you have found the right people to assist you, and if you have successfully imparted your vision to them, you should not need things done in a regimented fashion. You should trust your staff, have confidence in them, believing them to be men and women of God.

While I am going to know the overall character of everything that is going on in the church, there are many specifics that I know very little about, and some things I will never know anything about, because I don't need to. I have given that responsibility to the staff members. At the same time, they know their limitations. They know the lines they are not to cross and how far they can go without consulting me. A leader should draw definite lines and instruct his people in what they are. They need to understand the structure that surrounds their responsibilities and the limitations of their authority. That is all part of the delegation process.

Good people won't cross those lines. When they arrive at a line, they should consult you before going further. Usually my staff members already know what I am going to say or what I am going to do, but they are going to let me say it and let me do it. Outside of those guidelines, however, they realize their responsibilities I have given them and are free to fulfill them in their own ways. This is the process of leadership taking charge without taking over.

CHAPTER SEVEN

Submission to Authority

A leader can find good people who are qualified, gifted, and loaded with abilities. He can impart his vision, delegate authority, and allow them the freedom to express their gifts. But unless he understands the Godly principles of how to function in the realm of authority both as a follower and as a leader, then he is going to have difficulty all the days of his life. Authority assumes many forms. There is the authority of man in the earth, the authority of the church, the authority of civil government, the head of families, and more.

What Is Authority?

Authority is one of the least understood and most abused powers that we have. Many people resent and fear authority, and there are many who rebel against it. To be honest, because of the perverted nature of the world's system, most people are at the very least weary of authority. We all tend to look at it suspiciously. This general attitude usually has nothing to do with the integrity of the persons involved, either those who are suspicious or those who are honest. It has everything to do with the perverse nature of the world system in which we live.

Anyone who has lived long at all has experienced the abuse of someone else's authority. There is not a single person who has not been wrongly used or abused by someone in authority. This is what has brought about the suspicious attitude.

God never intended for authority to be represented in this light. All authority originates with God. For example, the Bible tells us that the devil is the god of this world, the prince of the power of the air. As such, he has a certain authority. The very authority that he has, as strange as it may seem to us, originated in God. Although the authority originated *in* God, it was not given to the devil *by* God. Rather, we are told in Genesis 1:26-28 that God gave this authority to man.

> *26 And God said, Let us make man in our image, after our likeness: and let them have dominion over the fish of the sea, and over the fowl of the air, and over the cattle, and over the earth, and over every creeping thing that creepeth upon the earth.*
>
> *27 So God created man in his own image, in the image of God created he him; male and female created he them.*
>
> *28 And God blessed them, and God said unto them, Be fruitful, and multiply, and replenish the earth, and subdue it: and have dominion over the fish of the sea, and over the fowl of the air, and over every living thing that moveth upon the earth.*

First, God created the earth, and by being the Creator, that automatically established His authority over the earth. God had creative authority over the universe, over the earth, and everything that was in and upon the earth.

Man Created Sovereign

Then He went further by creating a living being in His own image and after His own likeness--man, God's highest creation. And once created, God delegated to man His own authority over all the earth, giving him charge to bring everything into submission to himself. This word, *submission*, if not properly understood, can cause the hair on the back of your neck to stand up. The reason is because man is a sovereign being, with enormous God-given creative abilities, who is responsible to God for his own life and what he does with it.

In other words, every man is responsible for his own destiny. Responsible to whom? Responsible to his Creator. Therefore, the very idea of submission runs crosswise to his sovereignty. There is something inherent in every person that causes him to want to be the master of his own destiny, to direct his own life and make his own choices.

Because of this, if submission is misunderstood, man's sovereign nature will resist and can cause him to resent and rebel against all authority. When man stretches his sovereignty far enough, it can cause him to resent and rebel against all authority. What we need to understand is that God did not create authority for the purpose of domination. That's where the world misses it, both those who are in authority and those who are under it.

In Matthew, Chapter 8, the centurion came to Jesus on behalf of his servant who was lying sick and dying. Jesus said that He would go home with him and heal the man. The centurion refused, replying that he was not worthy, being a Gentile. He knew Jewish custom that declared that no Jew could go under the roof of a Gentile. Instead, he asked Jesus to just speak the word, and his servant would be healed, saying, "For I am a man under authority, having soldiers under me: and I say to this man, Go, and he goeth; and to another, Come, and he cometh; and to my servant, Do this, and he doeth it." That was the way he recognized Jesus' authority.

Most people would have insisted that Jesus come and literally put His hands on the servant, but the centurion was willing to believe in the power of authority more than he believed in the power of the flesh.

Purpose of Authority

God created authority for the purpose of blessing, not to cause divisiveness, abuse, domination, or control. Authority was never intended to be used for manipulation or dictatorial powers. Instead, it is to give those in authority the necessary power to fulfill their responsibilities. If that fulfillment of leadership responsibility is carried out, then blessings result.

Raw authority never brings blessing to anyone, nor does it bring curses or abuse. Instead, everything depends on how people use the power that the authority gives. In the King James version of the Bible, the Greek word for authority is power. Authority is the power to accomplish, or to be able to get those who are under this authority to do whatever is necessary in order to accomplish a desired result. Therein is the blessing.

A pastor, for example, has God-given responsibilities for the flock over which he has charge. The fulfillment of those responsibilities brings blessing to the flock. Also, a husband has responsibilities to his wife and children, and God holds him accountable for fulfilling those responsibilities. The writer of Hebrews tells us to submit to those who have headship over us because *they* must give account to God for us. The same is true in every area of leadership responsibility.

Every area of responsibility that a leader has is for the purpose of meeting a necessary need. This is what makes him a servant. The husband/father is there to serve the needs of his family. The pastor is there to serve the needs of the flock. The Chief Executive Officer of a corporation is there to serve the needs of that corporation and its personnel. The key that is required in fulfilling the responsibilities of authority, whether exercised by enforcement or relationship, is submission.

Role of Submission

Anyone in the position of leadership must have the submission of his followers in order for him to successfully fulfill his responsibilities. In leadership by enforcement, the power flows from the top down. For example, in the military, the general issues an order, and his subordinates pass that order right on down through the ranks and the order is carried out.

This is also true in a measure even in spiritual leadership. Orders still come from the top down. Jesus is the head of the church, and the authority in the church is ultimately exercised from His headship. It comes from Jesus to the Holy Spirit, to the five-fold ministry, right on down through the ranks of the church. The difference, however, is empowerment.

In natural leadership, the empowerment comes from enforcement from the top down, but in spiritual leadership, the empowerment comes through relationship from the bottom up. The leadership actually flows from the top down, but it is empowered from the bottom up through submission. When power flows from the top down, the farther it goes, the more it dissipates. When it flows from the bottom up, the higher it goes, and the stronger it becomes.

Headship of the Husband

The most powerful leaders are those who have the greatest degree of submission from those for whom they are responsible. The most powerful husband and father, the one who is able to accomplish the most for his family, is the one who has the highest level of submission from his family. God gives that husband/father the responsibility for his family and the authority that goes with that headship, but it is the authority to develop relationship, not to dominate.

In Ephesians 5:21, Paul likened the husband/wife relationship to Christ and the Church.

> *21 Submitting yourselves one to another in the fear of God.*

Here Paul is referring to both male and female. In Christ Jesus, there is neither male nor female, neither Jew nor Greek, bond nor free. Everyone is equal in the eyes of God. We are commanded to submit one to another, however, the leader is in no way seen as superior to the follower. The husband is not seen as superior to the wife and Christ is not even to be seen as superior to the Church. Christ and His Church are one. It is the Body of Christ. In the matter of relationship, there is no difference. In Ephesians 5:22-26, He explains the correlation between these two relationships.

22 Wives, submit yourselves unto your own husbands, as unto the Lord.

23 For the husband is the head of the wife, even as Christ is the head of the church: and he is the saviour of the body.

24 Therefore as the church is subject unto Christ, so let the wives be to their own husbands in every thing.

25 Husbands, love your wives, even as Christ also loved the church, and gave himself for it;

26 That he might sanctify and cleanse it with the washing of water by the word.

If the man has the responsibility of headship over his wife, if he has the headship responsibility, why then did Paul speak first to the wife rather than to the husband? If the man has the authority and responsibility, why didn't Paul speak to him first? It is because the power flows from the bottom up. It is impossible for the husband to exercise his headship responsibilities unless the wife empowers him to do so through her submission. The same is true with a pastor. He cannot exercise his pastoral responsibilities unless the congregation empowers him to do so through their submission because there is no enforcement ability.

If the husband does not understand these things, he, through frustration, or a feeling of inferiority, may declare himself the man of the house and demand submission. In doing so, he has abdicated his headship and reduced himself to the position of a natural leader rather than a spiritual leader. Once he has done that, the only thing he can do is resort to enforcement. Where is the blessing? Where is the harmony or unity? Where is the grace of God? The same is true in the church, in the workplace, or anywhere that authority is exercised.

If submission is misunderstood and exercised incorrectly, the results will be far different from God's plan. We must always remember that true submission is not a position of being debased by a leader, but rather it is a position of power.

The spiritual follower has enormous godly power at his disposal because he can choose to submit or he can choose to resist. If he resists, he weakens the power of the leader to fulfill his responsibilities. There is no greater power than the power of choice, and this is why these Scriptures speak first to the wife, who is representative of the follower.

The one who is ultimately in charge is the one who is *under* authority. The centurion understood that. He declared it himself, when he said, "I am under authority." Understanding this position gave him great power.

The question is often asked by wives, "Where should I draw the line? How far do I go in submission to my husband? In most cases, these are godly women whose husbands are many times not godly and not saved. These women are in an awkward position that requires them to compromise themselves. The answer is to submit to the husband to the fullest extent possible, but to draw the line where submission to the husband requires disobedience to God. This is true in all kinds of leadership/follower positions.

How far do you follow a leader? As Paul says, "Follow me as I follow Christ." We are never to follow a pastor or any other leader beyond his walk with God. If he is not following Christ then we are to stop following him in order to continue following Christ.

Paul exhorts wives to submit to their husbands as unto the Lord, and a congregation is to follow its pastor as he follows Christ. He explains that it is the follower's responsibility to submit in order to bring empowerment to the leader. The leader is told to take that empowerment and use it according to God's plan.

CHAPTER EIGHT

Love: The Motivating Factor

Once you understand the principles of submission to authority, you can understand the principles of exercising authority. There is a major difference, however, in how a believer exercises his authority over other believers, and how he exercises his authority over the world and its system.

Enforcing Authority

The world and its system are under the leadership of the devil. Through Jesus Christ, believers have been given authority over the devil and his system. Exercising authority over the enemy--the devil, his demons, and the curse--is completely different from exercising authority over believers.

First of all, because of the curse, the world is not going to willingly submit to leadership. The devil and his demons are not going to submit to the authority of the believer. They are rebellious by nature. Therefore, where sickness, and all other results of the curse, or the devil and his world system are concerned, the authority of the believer is going to have to be exercised through enforcement.

The Bible tells us that Jesus, through His death, burial, and resurrection, has destroyed the devil and his works.

Colossians 2:15 -- *And having spoiled principalities and powers, he made a shew of them openly, triumphing over them in it.*

Keep in mind that this was a *judicial* action, or a legal action, and for that reason, the devil is still on his throne for a period of time, though his time is short. He still possesses his authority over the world system and is still master of every unbeliever, but he has no authority over the believer. The moment a person believes on Jesus Christ, he is translated out of that kingdom of darkness over which Satan is god, into the Kingdom of Light over which Jesus is Lord. The authority that Jesus took back from the enemy becomes the believer's.

Man Given Dominion

Galatians 3:13 tells us that *"Christ hath redeemed us from the curse of the law."* We are no longer slaves to sin and death. Romans 8:2 says that *"the law of the Spirit of life in Christ Jesus hath made me free from the law of sin and death."* Satan, however, is a persistent cuss. He doesn't just quit and not bother us anymore. Because of his resistance anyone in spiritual leadership must use force. Satan's defeat must be enforced upon him and those under his power and control. We must take authority over sickness and disease by believing God and receiving by faith our healing, health, and abundance. We are to have dominion over the curse and the world--over everything except each other.

God has not given any believer dominion over another believer: authority, yes, but not dominion. We are under the dominion (or Lordship) of only One, the Lord Jesus Christ, and we are to rule and reign as priests. The Bible calls us kings and priests, or in some translations, a kingdom of priests.

God's Institutions: Home & Church

Within the kingdom of priests, there must be function. In order for there to be function, there must be organization. There are two institutions that God has created that He prizes the highest, and those are the home and the church. Because they are God's most prized organizations, they are the ones the devil fights the hardest to destroy.

The only way the devil has been able to reduce our nation and our society to the condition that it is in today is through an all out attack on the home. As long as the home is strong and intact, the society is strong and intact. If you are going to destroy society, you must destroy the home.

The church is salt and light. Without it, everything putrefies and dies. If you remove the church from society, the society will utterly self-destruct and judgment will fall. That's what happened to Sodom and Gomorrah.

Sodom and Gomorrah were as perverted and sin-filled as cities could get. You can't get any more debased than those two cities were. But that wasn't why God destroyed them. He destroyed them for lack of ten righteous people. It was the absence of righteousness that sealed the doom of those cities. God had agreed that if he could find just ten righteous people He would save the cities, but there was only one, and he was somewhat questionable. Those cities had reached that condition because of no salt or light.

That was the story of all of Canaan. God had to purge the entire country of its population. The Bible says that an unrighteous land will literally vomit out its inhabitants. That's what happened to Israel so the people were eventually scattered throughout the earth.

Leadership in the Home

When people grasp the concept of God's leadership plan, they do not chafe under it. They are able to channel their sovereignty constructively without feeling restricted or cut off. It is because of our sovereignty that God has structured leadership the way He has, empowering leadership through submission rather than through enforcement. The organization of the home is a marvelous concept.

Again, in Ephesians 5:22, God speaks first to the wife because she holds the power of how well that home is going to function as an organization. The enormity of the husband's responsibilities is described in verse 25, *"Husbands, love your wives, even as Christ also loved the church, and gave himself for it."*

Love is action. Just having love benefits no one but the person who has it, and then that is only limited. In order for love to be beneficial, it must be expressed through the act of giving oneself for another. Jesus so loved the church that He gave Himself for it. Husbands are to so love their wives that they will give themselves for her.

Jesus said greater love has no man than this, that he will lay down his life for his friends (author's paraphrase). Jesus literally did that, but this statement comes under the heading of the law of double reference--or having two meanings. First of all, Jesus literally laid His life down for His friends. He then told them essentially to do the same thing, but He wasn't commanding them to go to the cross or die literally, though some did. He was referring to the act of love--laying down your life for another. This is what makes the husband/wife relationship the most beneficial, and the most blessed.

This same principle holds throughout leadership. The primary responsibility of the wife or the one under leadership is to submit, but the primary responsibility of the leader is to love.

Love: Primary Responsibility of Leadership

What does love require? It requires everything. Love requires that we lay down our lives, as Jesus did so willingly for the joy that was set before Him. We see that joy described in Ephesians 5:26-32.

> *26 That he might sanctify and cleanse it with the washing of water by the word,*
>
> *27 That he might present it to himself a glorious church, not having spot, or wrinkle, or any such thing; but that it should be holy and without blemish.*
>
> *28 So ought men to love their wives as their own bodies. He that loveth his wife loveth himself.*

29 For no man ever yet hated his own flesh; but nourisheth and cherisheth it, even as the Lord the church:

30 For we are members of his body, of his flesh, and of his bones.

31 For this cause shall a man leave his father and mother, and shall be joined unto his wife, and they two shall be one flesh.

32 This is a great mystery: but I speak concerning Christ and the church.

The church functions through its relationship with Jesus Christ. To the extent that the church submits to the Lordship of Jesus, His blessings are poured out upon it. The submission to His headship enables Him to express His headship or leadership.

The same is true in the home. The wife's submission to the husband empowers him to bless her with all the responsibilities that he has. When we submit to authority in this manner, it is the authority to bless, not the authority to subdue or to have dominion over each other.

This is where men have missed it. Instead of going out and subduing the world as we have been commanded, bringing it into subjection, man has tried to bring other persons under his control. This is why conquerors and dictators never last. Victory for the perverted leader is always temporary. If you look back at every conqueror in history you will see that his victories or dominions were short-lived. Christ's victory is eternal.

Overcome Evil Through Submission

Overcoming evil through submission is so hard for the natural mind to accept. Jesus commanded us not to overcome evil with evil, but overcome evil with good. How did Jesus defeat evil? He defeated it by submitting Himself to it. You must understand how that worked. He didn't just lay down from the standpoint of total passiveness. That is not the way. Instead, He allowed evil to take its best shot. Then, when it had completed all it could do, accomplishing the full expression of death, placing Jesus in the very heart of the earth, into the pit of Hell itself, Jesus got up, walked out, and stripped evil of its authority in great triumph!

Through His death, burial, and resurrection, Jesus stripped the devil of the authority he had stolen from Adam. Jesus appeared to His disciples, who are representative of believers, and delegated that authority back to man as the authority of the believer. You see there is great power in submission if you understand it and know how to receive it.

The Under-Shepherd

Spiritual leaders always have leadership over those who belong to God, and therefore, are in some form an under-shepherd. For example, David was the king of Israel, but he was called the shepherd of God's people, the shepherd king.

The people of Israel were looked upon by David and by God as the flock of God under David's care. His primary responsibility was to love them. Every single thing that comes forth from a spiritual leader comes forth out of love.

In the structure of the local church, the pastor is the under-shepherd of the Lord's Headship and is responsible for the flock of God. He is first responsible to love his flock and out of this love to bring order, and to give direction. Jesus stated it simply, "Feed my sheep."

The primary way to feed the sheep is through the Word of God. That means the pastor must do exactly what Jesus did, preach and teach. The Word says that Jesus went about preaching, teaching and healing. Now healing encompasses every need of the spirit, soul, and body. The pastor is to cast out devils, counsel, minister, encourage, correct, exhort.

Paul exhorts young Timothy in pastoring his local church in 2 Timothy 4:1-2.

> *1 I charge thee therefore before God, and the Lord Jesus Christ, who shall judge the quick and the dead at his appearing and his kingdom;*
>
> *2 Preach the word; be instant in season, out of season; reprove, rebuke, exhort with all longsuffering and doctrine.*

Any kind of spiritual leadership demands patience, especially from pastors. It takes people time to grow and develop in the things of God. If you are an impatient person and are not long-suffering, then you will give up on people. We are never to give up on anyone as long as they live.

In order to be effective in preaching, teaching and ministry, authority must be exercised. The thing that impressed the people most about Jesus' teaching was that He taught with authority. It was not the authority to dominate, but the authority with which he taught--the authority of God. The man of God must speak and act with the authority of God, always motivated by love. Even Jesus' hard sayings were spoken through love. If the spiritual leader is motivated by self-interest, frustration, anxiety or fear, the power of God will not be present, and for that reason there will be no benefit to the people. The same is true with the husband in the home.

Husband: the Under-Shepherd of the Home

If the motivation of the husband is to do more for his wife than she can do for him, and her motivation is the same, there is no lovelier place to be. There has never been a case of two people walking in the love of God, ending up in a divorce court. Notice I said two people. It takes two. It is not enough for just the wife to walk in the love of God. That is surely better than neither of them, but that is not going to get the job done totally. Nor is it enough for just the husband to walk in the love of God. They must both stay in the love walk which means each of them laying down his life for the other.

The same is true in a church. If a pastor says that he is going to do more for his congregation than the congregation can ever do for him and continues to pour out his life for them, and the congregation submits to the authority of the pastor, then they will receive the blessings of God through him. This is the only way spiritual leadership can function.

CHAPTER NINE

Dealing With Your Enemies

One of the most unpleasant aspects of leadership is how to deal with your critics and your enemies. If you are a leader that accomplishes very much, you will have both. This is true in both natural and spiritual leadership. Enemies differ only by the type of leadership we hold.

In spiritual leadership, most of the enemies are also spiritual, and usually work through people. The devil and his demons seek out people through whom they can operate. Very often these people are not even aware that they are yielding to the enemy. Nevertheless, spiritual leaders must learn how to deal with criticism when it comes from people who oppose them.

There are successful ways to do that, and ways that are not so successful. The first thing that a leader is going to have to come to grips with is that he is not perfect. He must realize that he does not know everything and cannot do everything, nor is his way always the best.

Accept Your Imperfections

The leader who comes to the realization that there are others under his leadership that have more qualifications and understanding in some areas than he does, and who takes advantage of their knowledge, will be a far more successful leader than one who is insecure.

Insecurity will handicap a leader. For one thing, it will cause a leader to become too dependent upon himself in an effort to protect his leadership position. In so doing, he actually makes his position extremely vulnerable and often causes it to fail.

A good leader is one who knows how to lead qualified people to do what he needs to have done. There is a fine line between a leader maintaining his position of leadership while keeping his followers' respect of him, and being overprotective of his position of leadership and defensive of it. With that in mind, we need to realize that there are basically two kinds of criticism-- constructive and destructive.

Constructive Criticism

Very often your constructive critics can be among your greatest assets. Because a leader is not perfect, naturally not every decision he makes is going to be a right decision. When it is not, and if he is leading people of quality and ability, there will be some people among them who will recognize problems.

A constructive critic is almost always reluctant to say anything about what he sees wrong. Usually, he is someone who respects and honors the leader. However, his motive is to make things better, so his desire for the success in the endeavor will override his reluctance, and it should. He will then offer up constructive criticism, or criticism for the purpose of righting something or changing something for the better. Constructive critics are easy to deal with unless the leader is insecure.

If a leader is insecure or overly sensitive to criticism, he may see any form of criticism as a challenge to his leadership and immediately follow his first impulse, which is to become defensive. This is the worst thing that a leader can do. The moment he becomes defensive of his leadership is the moment he begins to lose it. Leaders need to be challenged by their critics, not threatened by them.

Destructive Criticism

Destructive critics, on the other hand, look for opportunities to voice what they think is wrong. The difference between destructive and constructive critics is motive. The motive of the destructive critic is always to destroy the leader. Almost one hundred percent of destructive criticism is born out of envy, spawned by the critic's desire to be in the leader's position. These people usually will not bring their criticism directly to you, but will voice it to other people instead.

How To React To Criticism

The first response a leader should have to criticism, regardless of whether it is constructive or destructive, is to hear it. Very often a leader, especially an insecure one, will not listen. He will cut the critic off even before he can express what he is trying to share. The leader will begin to defend his position. This kind of response is dangerous and destructive to his own leadership. The first thing you must do is listen. Hear what your critic has to say. If at all possible, don't even interrupt him. If the critic gets out of hand, of course you must deal with that, but under normal circumstances, whether the person's motive is right or wrong, listen to what he has to say completely. It is good just to let him get it off his chest, being able to express himself without feeling threatened or that he is bouncing up against a wall of defense.

Sometimes, however, when you sit silently and listen, your critic may begin to feel threatened, thinking that you are just waiting for an opportunity to jump on him. It is important to keep a non-threatening expression on your face and from time to time, encourage the person with a nod or a comment. Try to make your critic as comfortable as possible.

If the criticism is constructive, assure the person that you will do whatever is needed in order to correct the situation. If the criticism is wrong, but the motive is right, lack of information is involved. In this case, you can help your critic to understand that there are other things involved of which they are unaware. If you have the liberty, you can share those things. If not, assure your critic that the situation is under control and being handled properly.

Jesus said not to render evil for evil, but overcome evil with good. If it is constructive criticism, it is not evil. But if it is destructive, you must overcome it with good from a position of strength and security, not from a position of defensiveness.

The moment you go on the defensive, you have given the other person the advantage. There is a difference between defending yourself and having a defensive attitude. A defensive attitude is a negative attitude, and it always allows the other person the upper hand. The best defense is a good offense, so wait your turn. Don't interrupt. Don't put the person down or overpower him with your authority and position of leadership. In other words, don't intimidate him.

Very often leaders have stronger personalities than many of their followers. They learn how to use this to their advantage. There are times when it is appropriate, but not when you are under criticism. If you do overpower your critic, then you are not dealing with the situation, you are only covering it over and it will come up again.

After the critic has expressed himself, examine the criticism as impartially as you can to see if it is true. Very often you are going to find, especially in destructive criticism, that there will be an element of truth in the criticism that has been twisted to the critic's own advantage or perspective. This is what makes a destructive critic so dangerous. He will never be persuaded in his error. He will never be swayed off his opinion because his motive is not to correct a situation or a person, but to destroy him. Even so, you must hear the person out and examine his criticism for truth. Then address those parts that are true and valid, and explain that you will do what needs to be done to correct the situation in an appropriate manner.

The best way to handle a vicious, destructive critic is to never answer his criticism unless it is made in your presence. I have had people come into my office and rail and rant over something that has upset them. When this happens, you can seldom deal with that person's criticism, you must deal instead with the person. Jesus had a way of always going right to the heart of the problem, going after the root. When you deal with a destructive critic face-to-face, believe God to show you exactly what the heart of the problem is and deal with that. Sometimes you can redeem him and help him get past the problem that he has. If you can't, then pray for him.

I had a person come into my office one time with a list of things he perceived that I was doing wrong and ungodly in pastoring my church. He felt that these things were causing great damage to the church and congregation. He was irate. When he finished, I did not answer a single thing on his list. Not a one was valid or constructive.

This person's problem was not the way I was pastoring the church, but was in fact, his own inability to submit to any form of authority. He was as rebellious as anyone could be, refusing to be a team player. He wanted to be an individual performer and was unwilling to change. When people maintain this kind of attitude, they make the people around them and other players miserable.

On another occasion, a woman came into my office, raving at me. When she finished, I answered that I was sorry she felt the way she did. I said that I would like to help her, and asked if I could pray for her. She responded, "You can't pray for me!" and stormed out the door. I called her husband, knowing that he was aware she had been to see me, and asked for an appointment with him. I explained the problem to him because I wanted to help his wife. I was aware that his own life was miserable and shared some things that I felt might help him to help her through this situation.

He answered, "You are absolutely right, but I'm not going to do any of those things." I asked, "Why not?" He responded, "Because if I don't give in to her one hundred percent in everything she wants, she will leave me. She tells me that all the time, and I believe her. I want her, so I am not going to do anything you've suggested. I'll let her have her way." I answered, "Okay, God bless you. You can have her." They moved out of state, and to this day, nothing has changed. She is still under the power of a spirit of control.

Controlling Spirits

People who have controlling spirits can never serve you well in your position of leadership. Strong people can, yes. You want strong, gifted, intelligent people. You even want people with strong personalities, but what you do not want is controlling, manipulative people. You must know how to recognize controlling spirits. They will tear your organization to pieces every time, not just some of the time. If you put a person who has a controlling spirit in an area of responsibility under your leadership, they will destroy whatever they are around.

The sad part is that so very often, those are the people who are among the most gifted. Many times controlling, dominating, manipulative people have two complete sides. They have one side that draws people like a magnet and endears people to them. This is the side that allows them to get into position to do the damage that they do. The other side is just the opposite. It is full of domination, manipulation and control. You must realize you cannot recognize this side based on personality. You must discern it.

These people will get into your organization first by endearing themselves to you. They will work their way into positions of influence, and then will come around your backside to destroy you with destructive criticism. Many times it will happen before you even know that any of it is going on. They are very clever and deceptive.

I have dealt with a number of them. Usually they do not operate in established organizations because they cannot weave their way into them as easily as they can in young organizations that are establishing themselves. You will find that almost every new pioneer church will go through the exact same pattern of experiences.

In the early days of a ministry, along will come one, two, or more of these types of people, the controllers. They are after the new baby. They are there to capture the young, newborn for themselves, and many times, they succeed. It has happened in my church and I know very few pastors that have pioneered local works where it has not happened. Many times, unfortunately, it has destroyed the entire work. Some churches were salvaged. The church that I pastor was fortunate. We were able to recognize and deal with it and the damage wasn't permanent.

The way you deal with these people is by not playing their game. You will never change their thinking or convince them of your position, so don't even try. They are not interested. For every argument you give them against their position, they will take a new position. Moreover, they will take everything you say and turn it around, twist and pervert it, and use it against you. That is why you must never answer destuctive criticism.

I had one person, an influential member of our community, who went all over town telling everyone who would listen that I was a false prophet and warned them to stay away from my church. I never once answered that criticism. A lot of people came to me, asking if I knew what so-and-so was telling. I answered that I didn't think anything about it. That was between that person and God.

The worst thing a leader can do is to address criticism toward his leadership from his position of leadership. In a pastor's case, you must never try to answer your critics from the pulpit, or even worse, try to correct your critics from the pulpit. I have been in services where pastors have spent an entire service responding to criticism and correcting one person from the pulpit. That is not only nonsense, but is the most destructive thing you can do.

We had another situation in the early days of our church that created one of the greatest crisis in the area of leadership that I have ever gone through. Everything was in an uproar. A person, led by a controlling spirit, caused enormous damage. I never addressed the situation from the pulpit. I never addressed the individual about the criticism or answered it. A number of people came to me saying that as the pastor, I needed to deal with it because it was blatant. Ninety-nine percent of my dealing with it was between me and God in prayer. The other one percent was between me and the individual in private. Finally, it came to the place where I gave the individual an ultimatum--either repent and get her heart right, or leave. She chose the door.

The woman informed me that she was going to take the congregation with her. She said, "I can survive this. I don't know if you can or not. I don't think you can." I answered that we would find out who God had called, saying, "If God has called you, then the congregation will follow you. If He has called me, then they will follow me." The individual left and about six people followed. The rest stayed, and the church went on.

If I had gone to the pulpit and addressed the situation publicly, it would have caused a major church split. A significant number of people would have left the church and it would have taken years to recover.

When a church split occurs, it is almost never the pastor's fault, but is because he did not handle the situation properly. If he became defensive, he played into his critics' hands. You cannot fight the devil on his own territory. He will defeat you every time. You must deal with him from your position in the heavenlies.

You never find Jesus answering His critics. He never once defended Himself, not even among His disciples and His closest followers. In John 6:53-54, Jesus spoke to his followers about eating His flesh and drinking His blood. Of course, He was speaking spiritually, but they took Him literally.

The scriptures continue in verse 66, *"From that time many of his disciples went back, and walked no more with him."* Did Jesus then turn to His twelve disciples and say, *"Now wait a* minute, fellows. *Don't get upset. I know a lot of these people are leaving now, but let Me tell you what I was talking about."* No, He did not do that. He looked at them and asked if they were going to leave also.

This is the way God is. It is not that God is not willing to give an explanation. It is that God understands when no explanation is wanted because another motive is at hand. Anytime people sincerely wanted an explanation and came to Jesus, asking Him for an explanation, they got it. If these people who were offended had said, *"Lord, we don't understand that. Can you make it clearer and explain what you mean,"* He would have.

He would have answered them that the words He spoke were Spirit and life. He would have satisfied them even if He could not have given them full understanding at that moment. But they did not ask for an explanation. They yielded to offense. When people yield to offense, never try to correct it. Let them go. Their offense is in control, and as long as it is, they are going to follow their offense.

Understanding People

It is not easy to be a leader. It takes a lot of grace and supernatural understanding to be effective. What you must understand more than anything else about people, is people. You must understand human nature, or what makes folks tick.

When people came flocking to Jesus, praising and exalting Him, the scriptures tell us that He did not commit Himself to them, because He knew the heart of men. What that says is that Jesus understood human nature. He served the people, but He only committed Himself to God. As a leader, you must never commit yourself to people. Be committed on their behalf and be committed to God on their behalf, but never commit yourself to the people you serve. The devil understands human nature and he knows how to use it. If you commit yourself to people, then they will destroy you.

Ministries Under Attack

We have seen national ministries attacked by the news media and so-called "books of correction." Most of these ministries never answer their critics, regardless of what is said. The critics are not out to learn or to gain information. They are out to simply destroy.

You will notice that when the news media attacks a ministry that is truly in error, the ministry never survives. Many times this is God's judgment on that ministry. The scriptures tell us that if you judge yourself, you will not be judged. If you do not, God will judge His own people. Many times He uses the world to implement His judgment. We have seen a number of ministries go down as a result of criticism, but in those cases, the media proved to be right. On the other hand, when ministries of integrity come under criticism, the critics have never been able to touch them. Those ministries have gone right on. They continue to prosper. What is the difference? In these cases, the media is wrong.

Most men and women of God are ministers of character and integrity. They are God's anointed and you do not touch God's anointed. That does not mean that everything everyone has done has been correct, or that all of their decisions are right. All men of God have made errors in judgement in the things they have done, but their hearts were right. They believed at the time they were following God.

The bigger your ministry, the greater the impact of your leadership, the more exposed are your mistakes. The greater your successes, the bigger your mistakes. Everything is relative.

CHAPTER 10

Raising Up Leaders

The responsibilities of leadership go beyond the primary purpose of bringing order and giving direction. There is also the responsibility to train and develop other leaders in your service, or "raise up" leaders. The concept of multiplying yourself as described in a previous chapter is very important in ministry leadership. In secular businesses, training and developing leaders may not be necessary, but it is essential in the local church.

Concept of the Local Church

God created the local church to be a vital, growing, developing organism. The concept that has prevailed for a very long time in many circles is that a local church is a building that houses a relatively small number of people, one to two hundred, with a pastor and a few lay leaders to run it. Once you have that structure in place, the people just *go to church*. This concept is one of the reasons we have so many small churches with limited growth.

There is a big difference between *going to church* and *being a part of a church*. I believe and am convinced that God's intent is for churches to grow and develop. Everything to which God gives life is given the ability to grow. In order to sustain life, living things must grow and develop. Churches are no different. If churches are to grow and develop, it will obviously require the growth and development of leaders.

Helps Ministry Leaders

In church ministry, leaders are primarily ministerial leaders. The largest area of ministry in which most people will be involved is the Helps Ministry.

This ministry covers a wide spectrum of services. All manner of things come into this category. For example, the music ministry falls under the Helps Ministry, as do ushers, parking attendants, greeters, nursery workers, children and youth ministers, and on down the line.

When you have all of that responsibility, you must also have leadership to fulfill the responsibility. Those leaders must come from somewhere. They do not automatically show up but instead must be "raised up." Good senior leaders will be developers and trainers of people, raising them up to fulfill the responsibilities that God has given them. If the senior leader does not have the ability to do this, then he limits the size of his ministry. The time for a pastor or any other leader to start raising up leaders is when his organization is small.

Develop Before the Need

It may seem strange to you to start training leaders when you are small because there are few people for them to lead. If you have a vision for increase however, and plan to grow, then you must realize that you cannot train leaders as you *need* them, but rather as you have the opportunity to *develop* them. If you wait until you need them, then you are always going to be behind. You will become stressed out, and usually will end up cutting corners and putting people into positions that they are not developed and equipped to handle.

There are some things that a small church can do more easily than a large church. If a pioneer will take advantage of the opportunities that being small affords, it will surely benefit him in the years ahead when his organization increases. One of the greatest advantages that a leader has when his organization is small is time.

Redeeming the Time

A pastor usually starts out with just a few people, which allows him time to spend with them individually. Once a church reaches several hundred members, the ability and the opportunities become fewer and fewer. This is why you need to take advantage of your situation in the early stages of your growth. You begin by praying and searching among your people to see who has leadership *potential*, not necessarily who is a good leader.

At first glance, you may see no one in your congregation who is a good leader. What you are looking for are people that you can train and develop into good leaders. The people you choose may have never led anything, but that doesn't mean they do not have the ability to become good leaders.

Once you have identified leadership potential, you can begin to develop them. You do this by spending time with them, teaching them the Word of God, and training them in leadership principles. You can make strong leaders out of them.

Raising up leaders is one of the most needed and most neglected areas of leadership. The reason is that most leaders do not invest the time to do it. Also, the leader may feel threatened by a potential leader's ability. But, for the most part, the problem is time. A leader will use the excuse that he just doesn't have enough time. Ironically, one of the reasons a leader does not have enough time is because he does not have enough help, and by not taking the time to raise up leaders, he has limited his ability to increase.

There are many needs in the local church. Most people have no concept of what it takes to operate a ministry, and when a pastor is single-handedly trying to run the church, he cannot begin to cover the bases and meet the needs of the congregation.

People walk into church on Sunday mornings with no idea of what is involved in creating a meaningful church service. They take everything for granted without thinking about it. The sanctuary service is only one part of a network of activity going on. If a church is well organized and well structured with sufficient, trained and developed leadership, everything will come together so smoothly and efficiently that all the efforts are hardly noticed. That is the way it should be.

What people notice is what is not good. If your nurseries are not operating properly, you have havoc on your hands with parents and they will let you know in a hurry. Things will go wrong from time to time, but with properly trained leaders, you can keep mistakes to a minimal.

A young mother came to me in tears one day. Her family had visited another church in another city. It was a very large church with several thousand members. She was appalled over the condition of the children's ministry, and refused to leave her child in it because of the disarray. She was comparing it to her experience here at her home church. The church probably had a good children's program, but without good leadership, a good program is worthless.

Locating Leaders

Most spiritual leaders come up through the ranks, though it is not a laid-out, spiritual order of promotion in the ministry. In spiritual matters, promotion does not come from man, but from God.

Even though there is not a specified promotion system within the church that guarantees that as long as a person is successful in his position of leadership, he will be promoted to a greater one, nevertheless, that happens to many people. Many of the ministers on staff at Victory Fellowship came up through the ranks of the church.

For example, my first associate pastor was a layman in the church. When we were a very young church just getting started, he and his family joined. At the time, he was in the food service industry. After being a part of the church for a few years, he developed into some areas of spiritual leadership and eventually became our associate pastor.

Others have come up the same way, but they did not just happen to assume their positions. They had to be trained and developed into them. First and foremost, they had to be called to those ministry positions, but a call does not mean automatic success. When God calls, he equips, but that equipping must be developed.

Training People To Serve God, Not You

One of the things that a good leader must do is to train and develop people to the highest level of their ability, and then be willing to release them to the plan and purpose of God for their lives. Not everyone that you develop is going to remain with you. When that happens, you must not be selfish in thinking that because you have trained them and gotten them into position to be a benefit to you, they must stay. That is the wrong attitude. Still, it would amaze you how many pastors and leaders think that way. They look on it as a lack of loyalty and integrity.

I know one couple from another state who had come up through the ranks in their church. They were very gifted with children and possessed good leadership skills. Eventually, they were made the children's ministers and were successful. But they felt the need for further training and development. They believed they could get that at Rhema Bible Training Center, and had a keen desire to go. They felt that this was God's will. The pastor of their church did everything he could possibly do and think of to prevent them from leaving. He did not want to lose their services. He tried to talk them out of it, and when that didn't work, he tried to bribe them out of it. He even tried to intimidate them.

This pastor tried everything he could to keep these people from fulfilling what they had in their hearts to do. Eventually, their desire was so strong that they felt that they had to follow through. They turned in their resignation, but it still took a couple of extra years for them to break out of their situation. When they finally succeeded, there was much tension and adversity from the pastor toward them which caused hard feelings.

This man was trying to hold on to what he perceived to be his possession. These were *his* children's ministers. He had raised them and developed them. Anyone who maintains that kind of attitude as the senior leader, will eventually get to a situation where no one will want to work for him. People will not submit themselves to that kind of possessiveness. They need to be allowed the freedom to follow the plan of God for their lives.

In another situation, there was a pastor who came to Nashville to pioneer a church after he and his wife graduated from Rhema. They worked with their new church for several years, but it just never got off the ground the way he wanted it to. Over a period of time, he and his wife came to the conclusion that they had to lay it down and get some more training and developing.

After a lot of prayer and seeking God, they came to Victory Fellowship with their son and stayed for two and a half years. We gave them a wide open door to become involved in anything that they wanted to in the area of church ministry. They were free to take part in whatever they had on their hearts to help them learn more about the operation of a local church.

These were gifted people. I could have tried to lock them into an area of ministry in an effort to hold onto them. They were a tremendous asset and I could have found ways to make it very difficult for them to break away and follow the plan that God had put on their hearts. Instead, we helped them any way we could, giving them a lot of latitude to choose their own areas of development. Finally, the young man came to me and said that it would soon be time for them to go. I replied, "Fine, brother. We are for you." We began to talk about it a year before they actually left, and when they did, they went with our blessings.

During their last year, this pastor identified several areas in which he needed help--areas of organization and establishment. He asked if he could set up a Council of Advisors from among our own church leadership. Many pastors would have balked at that. They would have been intimidated for him to come into their churches in the first place, but they certainly would not have given him access to any of their leadership for fear that he would take them with him.

I told him to go ahead and pick out anyone he wanted and gave my blessing for them to serve him as long as he needed them. He picked out some of the strongest leadership that we had in the church. They served him for as long as the pastor needed them, and they are still at VFC. The whole purpose for raising leaders is for building the Kingdom of God.

In the 80's and 90's, we used to have a laymen's Bible School. We had churches in our area that sent people to our Bible

School by the van loads. Many pastors and their wives came. Some pastors would be uneasy for their people to come to another church's school, because of fear of losing them. We never, never encourage people to leave their church and come to VFC. The pastors whose people came to school ended up being blessed because they got their people back much more equipped to do the work of the ministry in own their churches.

Years ago, there was a church in town where the pastor fell into moral failure and the church closed down. One of the leaders of that church brought several families to Victory Fellowship. He told us up front that they were not planning to stay. "We want to come for a period of time to train and develop under your ministry," the leader said. "Then I want to take these families with me, if they want to go, and start another church with another pastor. We want to learn how to have the same strong, successful church that you have." I told them they were welcome to stay as long as they wished.

I must admit that when they got ready to go, I sensed in my spirit that they would have been better off not to leave, that it would be better for them to stay and become a part of this church. They could have been a great asset to the church, and I told them that. These people, unlike the other pastor, were not called to the ministry. They were lay people. But they desired to have an African - American pastor and an all African - American church so they could take the Word of Faith message to their particular community. I tried to keep them without being oppressive about it, but when they were determined to leave, I helped them find a pastor that fit what they were looking for. Through his ministry the church is doing well today. They have done far better because they received the time of development we offered.

As a leader, whether you are heading a department or leading a church, you *must not* train your people to serve *you*, or even to serve the church you are in, but rather, you must develop people to serve God and do what He has called them to do.

Spiritual Leaders: The Highest Call

Jesus laid down the standards for leadership through the demonstration of washing his disciples' feet. Leaders are appointed to serve. Although there are similarities in the roles of leadership in the natural and the spiritual, those in spiritual leadership have a higher call, and therefore must answer to a higher set of standards. To be an effective spiritual leader, you must know the standards, and then follow them. The highest order is love, giving of yourself to another. The purpose is to build the Kingdom of God, and the result is individual and corporate fulfillment of God's plan on earth.

CPSIA information can be obtained at www.ICGtesting.com
Printed in the USA
LVOW04s0827180815

450428LV00003B/4/P